DARE TO BELIEVE

Dare to Believe

~

SMITH WIGGLESWORTH

Compiled by
JUDITH COUCHMAN

Regal

From Gospel Light
Ventura, California, U.S.A.

PUBLISHED BY REGAL BOOKS
FROM GOSPEL LIGHT
VENTURA, CALIFORNIA, U.S.A.
PRINTED IN THE U.S.A.

Regal Books is a ministry of Gospel Light, a Christian publisher dedicated to serving the local church. We believe God's vision for Gospel Light is to provide church leaders with biblical, user-friendly materials that will help them evangelize, disciple and minister to children, youth and families.

It is our prayer that this Regal book will help you discover biblical truth for your own life and help you meet the needs of others. May God richly bless you.

For a free catalog of resources from Regal Books/Gospel Light, please call your Christian supplier or contact us at 1-800-4-GOSPEL *or* www.regalbooks.com.

Originally published by Servant Publications in 1997.

All Scripture quotations, unless otherwise indicated, are taken from the *King James Version*. Authorized King James Version.

Other versions used are
NIV—Scripture taken from the *Holy Bible, New International Version*®. Copyright © 1973, 1978, 1984 by International Bible Society. Used by permission of Zondervan Publishing House. All rights reserved.
RSV—From the *Revised Standard Version of the Bible*, copyright 1946, 1952, and 1971 by the Division of Christian Education of the National Council of the Churches of Christ in the U.S.A. Used by permission.

Cover design by Hile Illustration and Design

Library of Congress Cataloging-in-Publication Data
(Applied for)

    2 3 4 5 6 7 8 9 10 11 / 14 13 12 11 10 09 08 07 06

Rights for publishing this book in other languages are contracted by Gospel Light Worldwide, the international nonprofit ministry of Gospel Light. Gospel Light Worldwide also provides publishing and technical assistance to international publishers dedicated to producing Sunday School and Vacation Bible School curricula and books in the languages of the world. For additional information, visit www.gospellightworldwide.org; write to Gospel Light Worldwide, P.O. Box 3875, Ventura, CA 93006; or send an e-mail to info@gospellightworldwide.org.

For Mary Jane,
who dared to believe.

Contents

Acknowledgments

I AM GRATEFUL FOR the editorial team at Servant Publications who contributed to this book's development: Bert Ghezzi, Liz Heaney, Heidi Hess, and Traci Mullins. I'm also indebted to my sister, Shirley Honeywell, who contributed her typing skills to this project; and to Anne Scott, who cheered me on when it seemed I'd never finish.

As always, Charette Barta, Opal Couchman, Win Couchman, Madalene Harris, Karen Hilt, Shirley Honeywell, Mae Lammers, and Nancy Lemons deserve many thanks for their prayers as I worked on this book.

Introduction

"SMITH WHO?" I asked into the phone.

"Smith Wigglesworth," repeated my editor. "We want you to create a Life Messages book based on his teachings."

"Well, I'm not familiar with him, but Wigglesworth is certainly a *name* I won't forget," I said. You may not have heard of this remarkable preacher, either. But after you've read these forty devotionals based on his sermons, he is a *person* you won't forget.

While working on this book I've been reminded that God loves transforming ordinary people into extraordinary examples of faith and power. That was certainly the case with Smith Wigglesworth. At the turn of the century God captured Smith's soul, filled him with the Spirit, and embarked the uneducated plumber on a worldwide ministry of evangelism and healing.

Whatever skeptics may think of Smith's claim to miraculous healings, they can't deny the evangelist's love for the Word of God and his constant teaching about total surrender and obedience to Christ. Throughout his sermons, Smith balanced his advice to "only believe" and "have faith" with reminders to hear and follow God by reading the Bible and listening for His voice.

With this foundation, Smith then dared us to believe. He taught, "The Word of God is eternal and cannot be broken. You cannot improve on the Word of God, for it is life and it produces life. If you dare to believe, it is powerful. God wants us to be powerful, a people of faith, a purified people, a people who will launch out in God and dare to trust Him in glorious faith which always takes us beyond that which is commonplace to an abiding place in God."[1]

Wherever Smith traveled, he unabashedly promoted the Word of God and its power to heal. He told this story: "One day I was traveling in a railway train where there were two sick people in the car, a mother and her daughter. I said to them, 'Look, I've something in this bag that will cure every case in the world. It has never been known to fail.'

"They became very much interested, and I went on telling them more about this remedy that has never failed to remove disease and sickness. At last they summoned up courage to ask for a dose.

"So I opened my bag, took out my Bible, and read the verse, 'I am the Lord that healeth thee.' It never fails. He will heal you if you dare believe Him. People are searching everywhere today for things with which they can heal themselves, and they ignore the fact that the Balm of Gilead is within easy reach.

"As I talked about this wonderful Physician, the faith of both mother and daughter went out toward Him, and He healed them both, right on the train."[2]

In 1947 Wigglesworth, in perfect health, died at age 87. The doctor who examined Smith said, "What a fine specimen of manhood! There is no visible cause of death. It is just like a workman coming home from his work, taking off his coat and settling down to rest." It was an apt parting for a man who dared to believe.[3]

Judith Couchman,
July, 1996

1. Smith Wigglesworth, *The Anointing of His Spirit* (Ann Arbor, Mich.: Servant, 1994), 30.

2. Smith Wigglesworth, *Faith That Prevails* (Springfield, Mo.: Gospel, 1993), 21-22.

3. Albert Hibbert, *Smith Wigglesworth: The Secret of His Power* (Tulsa, Okla.: Harrison House, 1983), 16.

PART ONE

LIVING BY FAITH

This dear brother came to me one day and said,
"The doctor says this is the last day that my wife has to live."
I felt the Lord would heal his wife, so I asked another believer
if he would accompany me in praying for this dying woman.
When we entered the house, I asked the man with me to pray first.
He cried in desperation and prayed that this minister would be comforted
after he was left with motherless children.

I could hardly wait until he finished. What was the matter with him?
He was looking at the dying woman instead of looking to God.
You can never pray the prayer of faith
if you look at the person who is needing it.
There is only one place to look and that is to Jesus.

Rather than pray myself, I rushed to the bed,
picked up the bottle of oil, and poured the contents on the woman.
I said to her, "Woman, Jesus Christ makes you whole."
And she was not only healed, but was raised up that very hour.

THE ANOINTING OF HIS SPIRIT

SMITH WIGGLESWORTH'S INSIGHT
When we fix our eyes on Jesus, we can live by faith.

DAY 1

WHAT IS FAITH?

THOUGHT FOR TODAY

Faith is the Word of God living in us.

WISDOM FROM SCRIPTURE

So do not throw away your confidence; it will be richly rewarded.

You need to persevere so that when you have done the will of God, you will receive what he has promised.

For in just a very little while, "He who is coming will come and will not delay. But my righteous one will live by faith. And if he shrinks back, I will not be pleased with him."

But we are not of those who shrink back and are destroyed, but of those who believe and are saved.

Now faith is being sure of what we hope for and certain of what we do not see.

This is what the ancients were commended for.

HEBREWS 10:35–11:2, NIV

INSIGHTS FROM SMITH WIGGLESWORTH

How great should be our faith, for we cannot be saved except by faith; we cannot be kept but by faith; we can be baptized only by faith; and we will be caught up by faith.

Therefore, what a blessed reality is faith in the living God.

What is faith? Faith is the very nature of God. It is the Word of God. It is the personal, inward flow of divine favor which moves in every fiber of our being until our whole nature is so quickened that we live by faith, we move by faith, and we are going to be caught up to glory by faith, for "faith is the victory."

Faith is the glorious knowledge of a personal Presence within you, changing you from strength to strength, from glory to glory, until you get to the place where you walk with God, and where God thinks and speaks through you by the power of the Holy Spirit. Oh, it is grand; it is glorious!

God wants us to have far more than what we can handle and see, so He speaks of the substance of things hoped for, the evidence of things not seen. But with the eye of faith, we may see it in all its beauty and grandeur. God's Word is from everlasting to everlasting, and "faith is the substance."

If I should give some of you a piece of cloth, scissors, needle, and thread, you could produce a garment. Why? Because you would have the material. If I should provide some of you with wood, saw, hammer, and nails, you could produce a box. Why? Because you would have the material. But God, without materials, spoke the Word and produced this world with all its beauty. There was no material there, but the Word of God called it into being by His creative force.

Likewise, if you are begotten by this incorruptible Word, which lives and abides forever, you know that within you is this living, definite hope, greater than yourself, more powerful than any dynamic force in the world, for faith works in you by the power of the new creation of God in Christ Jesus.

Therefore, with the audacity of faith we should throw ourselves into the omnipotence of God's divine plan, for God has said, "All things are possible to him that believeth" (Mk 9:23). It is possible for the power of God to be so manifest in your human life that you will never be as you were before; for you will be ever going forward, from victory to victory, for faith knows no defeat.

The Word of God will bring you into a wonderful place of

rest in faith. God intends that you have a clear conception of what faith is, how faith came, and how it remains. Faith is in the divine plan, for it brings you to the open door, for you cannot open the door. It is God who does it, but He wants you to be ready to step in and claim His promises of all the divine manifestation of power in the name of Christ Jesus. It is only thus that you will be able to meet and conquer the enemy, for "greater is he that is in you, than he that is in the world" (1 Jn 4:4).

Living faith brings glorious power and personality. It gives divine ability, for by faith Christ is manifested in your mortal flesh by the Word of God. I would not have you miss the knowledge that you have heard from God, and to realize that He has so changed you that all weakness, fear, inability–everything that has made you a failure—has passed away. Faith has the power to make you what God wants you to be; only you must be ready to step into the plan and believe His Word.

The first manifestation of God's plan was the Cross of Calvary. You may refuse it; you may resist it. But God, who loves you with an everlasting love, has followed you through life, and will follow you with His great grace, that He may bring you to a knowledge of this great salvation.

God, in His own plan for your eternal good, may have brought something into your life which is distasteful, something that is causing you to feel desperate, to feel that your life is worthless. What does it mean? It means that the Spirit of God is showing you your own weakness so you might cry out to Him. And when you do, He will show you the cross of redemption. Then God will give you faith to believe, for faith is the gift of God.

Faith is an increasing position, always triumphant. It is not a place of poverty but of wealth. If you live in fruitfulness, you will have plenty. In Hebrews 11:2 it says, "The elders obtained a good report." The person who lives in faith always has a good report. The Acts of the Apostles was written because the lives of the apostles bore the fruit of active faith. To them faith was an everyday fact. If your life is in the divine order, you will not only have living, active faith but you will be building up someone else in faith.

Beloved, even with all the faith we have, we are not even so much as touching the hem of God's plan for us. It is like going to the seashore and dipping your toe into the water, with the great, vast ocean before you. God wants us to rise on the bosom of the tide and quit paddling along the shore. Oh, to be connected with the sublime power, that human nature may know God and the glory of the manifestation of Christ!

The Word of God is eternal and cannot be broken. You cannot improve on the Word of God, for it is life and it produces life. If you dare to believe, it is powerful. God wants us to be powerful, a people of faith, a purified people, a people who will launch out in God and dare to trust Him in glorious faith which always takes us beyond that which is commonplace to an abiding place in God.

The Anointing of His Spirit

QUESTIONS TO CONSIDER
1. Do you have the "audacity of faith" mentioned in today's reading? Why, or why not?
2. How can you increase your faith in God and His Word?

A PRAYERFUL RESPONSE
Lord, teach me to live each day by Your faith. Amen.

BY FAITH ALONE

THOUGHT FOR TODAY

Faith is the path to God's spiritual treasures.

WISDOM FROM SCRIPTURE

By faith we understand that the universe was formed at God's command, so that what is seen was not made out of what was visible.

By faith Abel offered God a better sacrifice than Cain did. By faith he was commended as a righteous man, when God spoke well of his offerings. And by faith he still speaks, even though he is dead.

By faith Enoch was taken from this life, so that he did not experience death; he could not be found, because God had taken him away. For before he was taken, he was commended as one who pleased God.

And without faith it is impossible to please God, because anyone who comes to him must believe that he exists and that he rewards those who earnestly seek him.

By faith Noah, when warned about things not yet seen, in holy fear built an ark to save his family. By his faith he condemned the world and became heir of the righteousness that comes by faith.

By faith Abraham, when called to go to a place he would later receive as his inheritance, obeyed and went, even though he did not know where he was going.

By faith he made his home in the promised land like a stranger in a foreign country; he lived in tents, as did Isaac and Jacob, who were heirs with him of the same promise.

For he was looking forward to the city with foundations, whose architect and builder is God.

By faith Abraham, even though he was past age and Sarah herself was barren, was enabled to become a father because he considered him faithful who had made the promise.

HEBREWS 11:3-11, NIV

INSIGHTS FROM SMITH WIGGLESWORTH

I believe there is only one way to all the treasures of God, and that is the way of faith. By faith and faith alone do we enter into a knowledge of the attributes, become partakers of the beatitudes, and participate in the glories of our ascended Lord. All His promises are Yea and Amen to them who believe.

God would have us come to Him by His own way. That is through the open door of grace. A way has been made. It is a beautiful way, and all His saints can enter in by this way and find rest. I find all is failure that is not based on the Rock, Christ Jesus. He is the Way, the Truth, and the Life. The way of faith is the way of Christ: receiving Him in His fullness and walking in Him; receiving His quickening life that fills, moves, and changes us; bringing us to a place where there is always an Amen in our hearts to the will of God.

Zacharias and Elizabeth surely wanted a son, but even when the angel came and told Zacharias he should have a son, he was full of unbelief. And the angel said, "Thou shalt be dumb,... because thou believest not my words" (Lk 1:20). But look at Mary. When the angel came to her, Mary said, "Be it unto me according to Thy word." It was her Amen to the will of God. And God wants us with an Amen in our lives, an inward Amen, a mighty moving Amen, a God-inspired Amen, which says, "It is, because God has spoken. It cannot be otherwise. It is impossible to be otherwise."

There are two kinds of faith. There is natural faith, but supernatural faith is the gift of God. In Acts 26:19, Paul told Agrippa what the Lord said to him in commissioning him. He said Paul's mission was "to open their eyes, and to turn them from darkness to light, and from the power of Satan unto God, that they may receive forgiveness of sins, and a place among those who are sanctified by faith in Me."

Is that the faith of Paul? No, it is the faith that the Holy Spirit is giving. It is the faith that He brings to us as we press in and on with God. I want to put before you this difference between our faith and the faith of Jesus. Our faith comes to an end. Most people in this place have come to where they have said, "Lord, I can go no further. I have used all the faith I have, and I have to just stop now and wait."

I remember going around to see some sick people. I was taken into a house where there was a young woman lying on a bed, a very helpless case. Her reasoning had gone, and many things were manifested there which were Satanic and I knew it. She was only a young woman, a beautiful child. The husband, quite a young man, came in with the baby, and he leaned over to kiss his wife. The moment he did, she threw herself over on the other side, just as a lunatic would do.

This was very heartbreaking. Then he took the baby and pressed the baby's lips to its mother. Again another wild thing happened. I asked one who was attending her, "Have you anybody to help?"

"Oh," they said, "we have had everything."

"But," I said, "have you no spiritual help?"

Her husband stormed out, saying, "Help? You think that we believe in God, after we have had seven weeks of no sleep and maniac conditions?"

Then with my faith I began to penetrate the heavens, and I was soon out of that house, for I never saw a man get anything from God who prayed on the earth. If you get anything from God, you will have to pray in heaven; for it is all there. If you are living in the earth's realm and expecting things from heaven, they will never come.

I said, "Come out of her, in the name of Jesus!" And she rolled over and fell asleep and wakened in fourteen hours perfectly sane and whole.

In 1 Corinthians 15:43 we read of the body being "sown in weakness," to be raised in power. It seems to me the Lord would have us know something of that power now, and would have us kept in that power, so that we shall not be sown in weakness.

There is one thing God has given me from my youth: a taste and relish for my Bible. I can say before God I have never read a book but my Bible, so I know nothing about books. It seems best to use the Book of books for food for your soul, for the strengthening of your faith, and the building up of your character in God, so that all the time you are being changed and made fit to walk with God.

Hebrews 11:6 says, "Without faith it is impossible to please Him: for he that cometh to God must believe that He is, and that He is a rewarder of them that diligently seek Him." God has something better for you than you have ever had in the past. Come out into all the fullness of faith and power and life and victory that He is willing to provide, as you forget the things of the past, and press on for the prize of His high calling in Christ Jesus.

Faith That Prevails

QUESTIONS TO CONSIDER

1. What, specifically, might be keeping you from living in the fullness of faith?
2. How can you say Amen to God's will for your life?

A Prayerful Response

Lord, I say Amen to Your will for my life. Fill me with Your faith. Amen.

A PRECIOUS FAITH

THOUGHT FOR TODAY

Faith from God is available to anyone who asks for it.

WISDOM FROM SCRIPTURE

Simon Peter, a servant and apostle of Jesus Christ,

To those who through the righteousness of our God and Savior Jesus Christ have received a faith as precious as ours: Grace and peace be yours in abundance through the knowledge of God and of Jesus our Lord.

His divine power has given us everything we need for life and godliness through our knowledge of him who called us by his own glory and goodness.

Through these he has given us his very great and precious promises, so that through them you may participate in the divine nature and escape the corruption in the world caused by evil desires.

For this very reason, make every effort to add to your faith goodness; and to goodness, knowledge; and to knowledge, self-control; and to self-control, perseverance; and to perseverance, godliness; and to godliness, brotherly kindness; and to brotherly kindness, love.

For if you possess these qualities in increasing measure, they will keep you from being ineffective and unproductive in your knowledge of our Lord Jesus Christ.

2 PETER 1:1-8, NIV

INSIGHTS FROM SMITH WIGGLESWORTH

This precious faith that Peter is writing about is a gift that God is willing to give to all of us. I believe God wants us to receive it so we may subdue kingdoms, work righteousness, and if the time comes, shut the mouths of lions. Under all circumstances we should be able to triumph, because we have no confidence in ourselves, but our confidence is only in God.

This precious faith is for all. But there may be some hindrance in your life that God will have to deal with. There is no other way into the power of God. God will do for us abundantly above all we ask or think when we can say with Paul, "I live no longer, and another, even Christ, has taken the reins and the rule" (Gal 2:20).

As this precious faith becomes a part of you, you will dare to do anything. And remember, God wants daring people—people who will dare all, people who will be strong in Him and dare to do exploits.

How shall we reach this plane of faith? Let go of your own thoughts and take the thoughts of God, the Word of God. If you build yourself on imaginations you will go wrong. You have the Word of God, and it is enough. And truly the Word of God changes a person until he becomes an epistle of God. It transforms his mind, changes his character, moves him on from grace to grace, makes him an inheritor of the very nature of God. God comes in, dwells in, walks in, talks through, and sups with him who opens his being to the Word of God and receives the Spirit who inspired it.

When I was traveling to New Zealand and Australia, there was an Indian doctor riding in the same car with me to the docks. He was very quiet and took in things that were said on the ship. I began to preach, of course, and the Lord began to work among the people.

In a second-class part of the ship there was a young man and his wife who were attendants for a lady and gentleman in the first-class section. As these two young people heard me talking to them privately and otherwise, they were impressed. Then the lady they were attending got very sick. In her sickness and loneliness she could find no relief. They called in the doctor, and the doctor gave her no hope.

And then, when in this strange dilemma—she was a great Christian Scientist, a preacher of it, and had gone up and down preaching it—they thought of me. Knowing the conditions, and what she lived for, that it was late in the day, that in the condition of her mind she could only receive the simplest word, I said to her, "Now you are very sick, and I won't talk to you about anything save this: I will pray for you in the name of Jesus, and the moment I pray you will be healed." And the moment I prayed she was healed. That was precious faith in operation.

Then she was disturbed. I could have poured in oil very soon; instead I poured in all the bitter drugs possible, for three days. I revealed her terrible state, and pointed out all her folly and the fallacy of her beliefs.

She became so penitent and brokenhearted. The thing that struck her first was that she had to preach the simple gospel of Christ instead of Christian Science. She asked me if she had to give up certain things. I won't mention the things; they are too vile. I said, "What you have to do is see Jesus and take Jesus." When she saw the Lord in His purity, the other things had to go. At the presence of Jesus all else goes.

This opened the door. I had to preach to all on the boat. As I preached, the power of God fell, conviction came, and sinners were saved. They followed me into my cabin one after another. God was working there.

Then this Indian doctor came. He said, "What shall I do? I cannot use medicine any more. Your preaching has changed me. But I must have a foundation. Will you spend some time with me?"

As we spent time alone together, God broke the fallow ground. This Indian doctor was going back to his Indian conditions under a new order. He told me of the great practice he had. He was going back to his practice to preach Jesus.

If you have lost your hunger for God, if you do not have a cry for more of God, you are missing the plan. There must come up from you a cry that cannot be satisfied with anything but God. He wants to give you the vision of what is ahead, of something higher than you have ever attained.

If you ever stop at any point, pick up at the place where you dropped through, and begin again under the refining light and power of heaven; God will meet you. And while He will bring you to a consciousness of your own frailty and to a brokenness of spirit, your faith will lay hold of Him and all the divine resources. His light and compassion will be manifested through you, and He will send the rain.

Shall we not dedicate ourselves afresh to God? Some say, "I dedicated myself last night to God." But every new revelation brings a new dedication. Let us seek Him.

Faith That Prevails

QUESTIONS TO CONSIDER
1. Have you lost your hunger for God? How can you get it back?
2. What new revelation about faith is God showing you?

A PRAYERFUL RESPONSE
Lord, increase my hunger for You and Your precious faith. Amen.

DAY 4

DARE TO BELIEVE

THOUGHT FOR TODAY

When we base our faith on knowledge, we can believe in God's promises.

WISDOM FROM SCRIPTURE

Then they asked him, "What must we do to do the works God requires?"

Jesus answered, "The work of God is this: to believe in the one He has sent."

So they asked him, "What miraculous sign then will you give that we may see it and believe you? What will you do? Our forefathers ate the manna in the desert; as it is written: 'He gave them bread from heaven to eat.'"

Jesus said to them, "I tell you the truth, it is not Moses who has given you the bread from heaven, but it is my Father who gives you the true bread from heaven. For the bread of God is He who comes down from heaven and gives life to the world."

"Sir," they said, "from now on give us this bread."

Then Jesus declared, "I am the bread of life. He who comes to me will never go hungry, and he who believes in me will never be thirsty.

"But as I told you, you have seen me and still you do not believe.

"All that the Father gives me will come to me, and whoever comes to me I will never drive away.

"For I have come down from heaven not to do my will but to do the will of him who sent me."

JOHN 6:28-38, NIV

Nothing in the world glorifies God so much as simple faith in what God's Word says. Jesus said, "My Father works and I work" (Jn 5:17). He saw the way the Father did the works; it was on the groundwork of knowledge, a faith based upon knowledge.

When I know Him, I can lay hold of His promises. There is no struggle, "for every one that asketh receiveth; and he that seeketh findeth; and to him that knocketh it shall be opened" (Mt 7:8). Jesus lived to manifest God's glory on the earth, to show what his Father was like, that many sons might be brought to glory (Heb 2:10). John the Baptist came as a forerunner, testifying beforehand to the coming revelation of the Son. The Son came, and in the power of the Holy Spirit revealed faith. The power is not of us, but of God. Yes, beloved, it is the power of Another within us.

Jesus said, "The works that I do shall [you] do also" (Jn 14:12). Oh, the joy of the knowledge of it! To know Him. As we look back, we see how God has brought us through in His love and we can shout hallelujah. When pressed beyond measure by the Spirit, God brings us face to face with reality. We must know the sovereignty of His grace and the manifestation of His power—His blessed Holy Spirit dwelling in us and manifesting His works.

Where am I? I am in Christ; He is in God, and in the Holy Spirit, the great revealer of the Son. Three persons dwelling in humankind. The Spirit works in righteousness, bringing us to the place where all unbelief is dethroned and Christ is made the head of the corner. Here is a glorious fact: We are in God's presence, possessed by Him. We are not our own; we are clothed with Another.

What for? For the deliverance of the people.

Many can testify to the day and hour when they were delivered from sickness by a supernatural power. Some would have passed away with influenza if God had not intervened. But God stepped in with a new revelation, showing us that we are born from above, born by a new power, God dwelling in us and superseding the old. Jesus said, "If ye shall ask anything in My name, I will do it" (Jn 14:14). Ask and receive, and your joy shall be full, if you dare to believe. God is more eager to answer than we are to ask. I am speaking of faith based upon knowledge. I was healed of appendicitis because of faith based upon knowledge of that experience. Where I have ministered to others, God has met and answered according to His will. It is in our trust and knowledge that God will not fail us if we will only believe.

The centurion told Jesus, "Speak the word only, and my servant shall be healed." Jesus said to the centurion, "'Go thy way; and as thou hast believed, so be it done unto thee.' And his servant was healed in the selfsame hour" (Mt 8:8, 13).

In one place where I was staying, a young man told us that his sweetheart was dying; there was no hope.

I said, "Only believe."

What was it? Faith based upon knowledge. I knew that what God had done for me, He could do for her. We went into the house. Her sufferings were terrible to witness. I said, "In the name of Jesus, come out of her."

The girl cried, "Mother, Mother, I am well!" Then I said the only way to make us believe was for her to get up and dress. Presently she came downstairs, dressed. The doctor came in and examined her carefully. He said, "This is of God; this is the finger of God." It was faith based upon knowledge of who He is.

If I received a check for a thousand dollars and knew only imperfectly the character of the person who sent it, I should be careful not to count on it until it was honored. Jesus did great works because of His knowledge of His Father. Faith begets knowledge, fellowship, communion. If you see imperfect faith—full of doubt, a wavering condition—it always comes of imperfect knowledge.

The crowd following Jesus asked Him, "What shall we do, that we might work the works of God?" Jesus answered, "This is the work of God, that ye believe on Him whom He hath sent" (Jn 6:28-29).

Anything else? Yes. He took our infirmities and healed all our diseases. I am a marvel of healing. If I fail to glorify God, the very stones would cry out.

Salvation is for all! Healing is for all! Baptism of the Holy Spirit is for all! Reckon yourself dead to sin, but alive to God. By His grace, get the victory every time. It is possible to live a holy life.   *The Anointing of His Spirit*

QUESTIONS TO CONSIDER
1. How can you be sure your faith is based on knowledge?
2. What will you dare to believe God for today?

A PRAYERFUL RESPONSE
Lord, I dare to believe in Your promises and marvelous works. Amen.

BUILDING ON THE WORD

THOUGHT FOR TODAY

God's Word is the unshakable foundation for faith.

WISDOM FROM SCRIPTURE

I will praise you, O LORD, with all my heart; before the "gods" I will sing your praise.

I will bow down toward your holy temple and will praise your name for your love and your faithfulness, for you have exalted above all things your name and your word.

When I called, you answered me; you made me bold and stouthearted.

May all the kings of the earth praise you, O LORD, when they hear the words of your mouth.

May they sing of the ways of the LORD, for the glory of the LORD is great.

Though the LORD is on high, he looks upon the lowly, but the proud he knows from afar.

Though I walk in the midst of trouble, you preserve my life; you stretch out your hand against the anger of my foes, with your right hand you save me.

The LORD will fulfill his purpose for me; your love, O LORD, endures forever—do not abandon the works of your hands.

PSALM 138, NIV

If you are going to progress in the divine life, you must have a real foundation, and there is no foundation apart from faith. If you are standing on the Rock, no powers can move you, and there is no establishment for you outside of God's Word. Everything else is sand.

If you build on anything else but the Word of God—on imaginations, sentimentality, feelings, or any special joy—it will mean nothing. You must have a foundation, and that foundation is the Word of God.

We are told that the Word of God shall stand forever, and not one jot or tittle of the Word shall fail. In Psalm 138 we read, "Thou hast magnified Thy name and Thy word above all" (verse 2). Also, in John 1:1-3, there is a wonderful word: "In the beginning was the Word, and the Word was with God, and the Word was God. The same was in the beginning with God. All things were made by Him, and without Him was not any thing made that was made."

Here we have the foundation of all things, which is the Word. It is a substance. It is a power. It is a personality. It is a divine injunction to every soul that enters into this privilege, to be born of this Word, to be created of this Word, to have knowledge of this Word.

It helps me to know that I am living in facts, I am moving in facts, I am in the knowledge of the principles of the Most High. God is a reality, and He is proving His mightiness in the midst of all of us. As we open ourselves to divine revelation and get rid of all things which are not of the Spirit, then we shall understand how mightily God can take us on in the Spirit and move the things which are and bring into prominence the things which are not.

Oh, the riches, the depths of the wisdom of the Most High! May He enlarge us. God wants us to be so devoted to

Him that He can unveil Himself. He rolls the clouds away; the mists depart at His presence. God is almighty in His movement. He has immensity of wisdom, unfolding the mysteries and the grandeur of His plan for the human race, that we may sink into insignificance, and that His mightiness may move upon us until we are the children of God with power.

Oh, this wonderful salvation! It is so beautiful.

What was the Word? The Word was Jesus. The Word became flesh and dwelt among us, and we saw and beheld the glory of God. That which was from the beginning, which we have heard, which we have seen with our eyes, which we have looked upon, and our hands have handled, the Word of life; (for the life was manifested, and we have seen it, and bear witness, and show unto you that eternal life, which was with the Father, and was manifested unto us). "That which we have seen and heard we declare unto you, that ye also may have fellowship with us: and truly our fellowship *is* with the Father, and with his Son Jesus Christ" (1 Jn 1:1-3).

Oh, beloved, Jesus is the Word. He is the revelation sent forth from God. All fullness dwells in Him. "Of his fulness have all we received, and grace for grace" (Jn 1:16). In weakness, strength; in poverty, wealth. This Word is a flame of fire! It may burn in your bones. It may move in every tissue of your life. Oh, the fact that I am begotten again and have become a child of God! Oh, how the whole creation groans for the manifestation of the children of God! How we need the Word. The Word is life.

We read about Jesus Christ our Lord, that He was "declared to be the Son of God with power" (Rom 1:4a). Sons must have power. We must have power with God and with our fellow creatures. We must have power over Satan, power over evil. You can never make evil pure. You cannot transform impurity into purity. The carnal mind is not subject to the will of God, and cannot be. It must be destroyed.

It is most necessary that we should have the vision of God. The people have perished when there has been no vision. God wants us to have visions, revelations, and manifestations. You cannot have the Holy Spirit without manifestations and revelations. We must live in an anointing, a power, a transformation, and a divine attainment where God becomes wholly enthroned.

God cast Satan out of heaven because of his pride. But God could not have cast him out if Satan had been His equal in power. We can never bind the strong man until we are in the place of binding. How was Satan cast out? By the Word of God's power. And if we get to know and understand the principle of our inheritance by faith, we shall find that Satan will always be cast out by the same power that cast him out in the beginning.

We need to eat and drink of this Word. We need to feed upon it in our hearts. We need a holy revelation that will take away the mist from our eyes and reveal Jesus. Don't forget that every day can be a day of advancement. If you have not made any advancement since yesterday, you are backsliding. There is only one direction for you between Calvary and glory, between your conversion and heaven, and it is forward.

We must catch the vision of the Master day by day. We must destroy everything that is not holy, for God wishes to see us on high. *The Anointing of His Spirit*

QUESTIONS TO CONSIDER

1. Are you content with your progress in reading God's Word? Why or why not?
2. What are you doing to ensure that your faith is building on God's Word?

A Prayerful Response

Lord, I will feed on Your Word to build my faith in You. Amen.

FAITH OR UNBELIEF?

THOUGHT FOR TODAY

Faith rooted in holy living casts out unbelief.

WISDOM FROM SCRIPTURE

Be patient, then, brothers, until the Lord's coming. See how the farmer waits for the land to yield its valuable crop and how patient he is for the autumn and spring rains.

You, too, be patient and stand firm, because the Lord's coming is near....

Brothers, as an example of patience in the face of suffering, take the prophets who spoke in the name of the Lord.

As you know, we consider blessed those who have persevered. You have heard of Job's perseverance and have seen what the Lord finally brought about. The Lord is full of compassion and mercy....

Is any one of you in trouble? He should pray. Is anyone happy? Let him sing songs of praise. Is any one of you sick? He should call the elders of the church to pray over him and anoint him with oil in the name of the Lord.

And the prayer offered in faith will make the sick person well; the Lord will raise him up. If he has sinned, he will be forgiven.

Therefore confess your sins to each other and pray for each other so that you may be healed. The prayer of a righteous man is powerful and effective.

Elijah was a man just like us. He prayed earnestly that it would not rain, and it did not rain on the land for three and a half years. Again he prayed, and the heavens gave rain, and the earth produced its crops.

JAMES 5:7-8, 10-11, 13-18, NIV

Faith is an inward operation of that divine power which dwells in the contrite heart, and which has power to lay hold of the things not seen. Faith is a divine act. Faith is God in the soul. God operates by His Son, and transforms the natural into the supernatural.

Faith is active, never dormant; faith lays hold; faith is the hand of God; faith is the power of God; faith never fears; faith lives amid the greatest conflict; faith is always active; faith moves even things that cannot be moved. God fills us with His divine power, and sin is dethroned. But you cannot live by faith until you are righteous. You cannot live by faith if you are unholy or dishonest.

The Lord was looking for fruit when He cursed the tree in Mark 11:11-15. He found nothing but leaves. There are thousands of people like that; they dress up like Christians but it is all leaves. "Herein is my Father glorified, that ye bear much fruit" (Jn 15:8). He has no way in which to get fruit except through us. We are not to be ordinary people. To be saved is to be extraordinary—an exposition of God.

When Jesus was talking about the new life He said, "Except a man be born of God, he cannot see the kingdom of God. That which is born of the flesh is flesh; and that which is born of the Spirit is spirit" (Jn 3:3, 6, RSV).

We must remember we have entered into the manifestation of the glory of God, and in that is great power and strength. Many people might have been far ahead of where they are today, if they had not doubted. If by any means the enemy can come in and make you believe a lie, he will do so. We have had to struggle to maintain our standing in our salvation, for the enemy would beat us out of that if possible.

In the closeness of and oneness with Christ there is no fear, but perfect confidence all the time. The child of God need not go back a day for this experience, for the presence of the Lord is with him, and the Holy Spirit is in him and in mighty power if he will believe. We should stir up one another and provoke one another to good works.

If we find that there is unbelief in us, we must search our hearts to see why it is there. Where there is a living faith, there is no unbelief, and we go on from faith to faith until it becomes natural to live there. But if you try to live by faith before you are justified by God, you will fail, for "the just shall live by faith" (Rom 1:17). When you are just, it is a natural consequence for you to live by faith. It is easy; it is joyful; it is more than that: it is our life and spiritual inheritance.

Elijah was a man with passions like ours. The sins of the people were grieving the heart of God, and the whole house of Ahab was in an evil state. But God moved upon this man Elijah and gave him an inward cry: "There shall not be dew nor rain these years, but according to my word" (1 Kgs 17:1). "And it rained not on the earth by the space of three years and six months" (Jas 5:17). "And when he prayed again the heaven gave rain, and the earth brought forth her fruit" (Jas 5:18).

The Bible asks, "Is any among you afflicted? Let him pray. Is any merry? Let him sing psalms. Is any sick among you? Let him call for the elders of the church; and let them pray over him, anointing him with oil in the name of the Lord: And the prayer of faith shall save the sick, and the Lord shall raise him up; and if he has committed sins, they shall be forgiven him. Confess your faults one to another, and pray one for another, that ye may be healed. The effectual fervent prayer of a righteous man availeth much" (Jas 5:13-16).

Do you want to have faith that cannot be denied? I have

learned if I dare put up my hands in faith, God will fill them. Come, seek God and let us get a touch of heaven today.

Only Believe!

Questions to Consider

1. How are you sometimes tempted toward unbelief?
2. What will you do to cast out this unbelief?

A Prayerful Response

Lord, I long for greater faith in You. Please forgive my unbelief. Amen.

Broken by God

Thought for Today

Brokenness before God increases our faith.

Wisdom from Scripture

Christ is the end of the law so that there may be righteousness for everyone who believes.

Moses describes in this way the righteousness that is by the law: "The man who does these things will live by them."

But the righteousness that is by faith says: "Do not say in your heart, 'Who will ascend into heaven?' (that is, to bring Christ down) or 'Who will descend into the deep?'" (that is, to bring Christ up from the dead).

But what does it say? "The word is near you; it is in your mouth and in your heart," that is, the word of faith we are proclaiming: That if you confess with your mouth, Jesus is Lord, and believe in your heart that God raised him from the dead, you will be saved.

For it is with your heart that you believe and are justified, and it is with your mouth that you confess and are saved.

As the Scripture says, "Anyone who trusts in him will never be put to shame."

For there is no difference between Jew and Gentile—the same Lord is Lord of all and richly blesses all who call on him, for, "Everyone who calls on the name of the Lord will be saved."

How, then, can they call on the one they have not believed in? And how can they believe in the one of whom they have not heard? And how can they hear without someone preaching to them?

And how can they preach unless they are sent? As it is written, "How beautiful are the feet of those who bring good news!"

But not all the Israelites accepted the good news. For Isaiah says, "Lord, who has believed our message?"

Consequently, faith comes from hearing the message, and the message is heard through the word of Christ.

ROMANS 10:4-17, NIV

INSIGHTS FROM SMITH WIGGLESWORTH

What makes us lose confidence is disobedience to God and His laws. Jesus said it was because of those who stood around that He prayed; He knew that God always heard Him. And because Jesus knew that His Father always heard Him, He knew that the dead could come forth.

At times there seems to be a stone wall in front of us. Everything seems as black as midnight, and there is nothing left but confidence in God. There is no feeling. What we must do is to have confidence to believe that He will not fail, indeed, cannot fail. We shall never get anywhere if we depend upon our feelings. There is something a thousand times better than feelings, and it is the naked Word of God.

There is a divine revelation within us that came in when we were born from above. To be born into the new kingdom is to be born into a new faith. Paul speaks of two classes of people: one is obedient and the other disobedient. The obedient always obey God when He first speaks. He will use them to make the world know there is a God.

We cannot talk about things we have never experienced. It seems to me that God has a process of training us. We cannot take people into the depths of God unless we have been broken ourselves. I have been broken and broken and broken. Praise God that He is near to those who are brokenhearted. We must be broken to get into the depths of God.

We fail to realize the largeness of our Father's measure, and we forget that He has a measure which cannot be exhausted. It pleases Him when we ask for more. How much more? It is the "much more" that God shows me. I see that God has a plan of healing. It requires perfect confidence in Him which comes from fellowship with Him. There is wonderful fellowship with Jesus. The chief thing is to be sure that we take time for our communion with Him. There is a communion with Jesus that is life, that is better than preaching. If God tells you definitely to do anything, do it, but be sure it is God who tells you.

I used to work with a man who had been a Baptist minister for twenty years. He was one of the sweetest souls I ever met. I used to walk by his side and listen to his instruction. God made the Word in his hand as a two-edged sword to me, and I used to say, "Yes, Lord." This man of God often pruned me with the sword of God, and it is just as sweet to me today as it was then.

If the sword ever comes to you, never straighten yourself up against it, but let it pierce you. You must be yielded to the Word of God. The Word will work out love in your heart, and when practical love is in your heart there is no room to vaunt yourself. You see yourself as nothing when you become lost in this divine love. I praise God for the sword that pierces us and for a tender conscience. We need to have hearts that are broken and melted by the love of God.

The Anointing of His Spirit

QUESTIONS TO CONSIDER

1. When has God broken you in the past? How did you respond?
2. Are you in need of brokenness today? If so, what can you do about it?

A PRAYERFUL RESPONSE

Lord, give me a heart that is broken and melted by Your love. Amen.

DAY 8

IF YOU WILL BELIEVE

THOUGHT FOR TODAY

If you will believe, all things are possible.

WISDOM FROM SCRIPTURE

In the morning, as they went along, they saw the fig tree withered from the roots.

Peter remembered and said to Jesus, "Rabbi, look! The fig tree you cursed has withered!"

"Have faith in God," Jesus answered.

"I tell you the truth, if anyone says to this mountain, 'Go, throw yourself into the sea,' and does not doubt in his heart but believes that what he says will happen, it will be done for him.

"Therefore I tell you, whatever you ask for in prayer, believe that you have received it, and it will be yours.

"And when you stand praying, if you hold anything against anyone, forgive him, so that your Father in heaven may forgive you your sins."

MARK 11:20-26, NIV

INSIGHTS FROM SMITH WIGGLESWORTH

Everywhere people are trying to discredit the Bible and take the miraculous from it. One preacher says, "Well, you know, Jesus arranged beforehand to have that colt tied where it was, and for the men to say just what they did." I tell you God can arrange everything without going near. He can plan for you, and when He plans for you, all is peace.

Another preacher said, "It was an easy thing for Jesus to feed the people with five loaves. The loaves were so big in those days that it was a simple matter to cut them into a thousand pieces each." But he forgot that one little boy brought those five loaves all the way in his lunch basket. There is nothing impossible with God. All the impossibility is with us when we measure God by the limitations of our unbelief. We have a wonderful God whose ways are past finding out and whose grace and power are limitless.

I was in Belfast one day and saw a man from the assembly. He said to me, "Wigglesworth, I am troubled. I have had a good deal of sorrow during the past five months. I had a woman in my assembly who could always pray the blessing of heaven down on our meetings. She is an old woman, but her presence is always an inspiration. But five months ago she fell and broke her thigh. The doctors put her into a plaster cast, and after five months they broke the cast. But the bones were not properly set, so she fell and broke the thigh again." ·

He took me to her house where she was lying in a bed on the right-hand side of the room. I said to her, "Well, what about it now?"

She said, "They have sent me home incurable. The doctors say I am so old that my bones won't knit. There is no nutriment in my bones and they cannot do anything for me; they say I shall have to lie in bed for the rest of my life."

I said to her, "Can you believe God?"

She replied, "Yes, ever since I heard you had come to Belfast my faith has been quickened. If you will pray, I will believe. I know there is no power on earth that can make the bones of my thigh knit, but I know there is nothing impossible with God."

I said, "Do you believe He will meet you now?"

She answered, "I do."

It is grand to see people believe God. God knew all about this leg and that it was broken in two places. I said to the woman, "When I pray, something will happen." Her husband was sitting there; he had been in his chair for four years and could not walk a step.

He called out, "I don't believe. I won't believe. You will never get me to believe."

I said, "All right," and laid my hands on his wife in the name of the Lord Jesus. The moment hands were laid upon her the power of God went through her and she cried out, "I'm healed!"

I said, "I'm not going to help you rise. God will do it all." She rose and walked up and down the room, praising God.

The old man was amazed at what had happened to his wife, and he cried out, "Make me walk, make me walk!"

I said to him, "You old sinner, repent."

He cried out, "Lord, You know I never meant what I said. You know I believe." I don't think he meant what he said; anyhow the Lord was full of compassion. If He marked our sins, where would any of us be?

I laid my hands on him and the power went right through the old man's body; and those legs, for the first time in four years, received power to carry his body, and he walked up and down and in and out. He said, "Oh, what great things God has done for us tonight!"

Desire toward God, and you will have desires from God. He will meet you on the line of those desires when you reach out in simple faith.

Did you believe before you were saved? So many people would be saved, but they want to feel saved first. There was never a person who felt saved before he believed. God's plan is always this: If we will believe, God wants to bring us all to a definite place of unswerving faith and confidence in Himself.

As an example of the power of faith, Jesus uses the figure

of a mountain. Why does He say a mountain? Because if faith can remove a mountain, it can remove anything. The plan of God is so marvelous that if we will only believe, all things are possible.

There is one special phrase to which I want to call your attention: "and shall not doubt in his heart" (Mt 21:21). The heart is the mainspring. What is a heart of love? A heart of faith. Faith and love are kin. God brings us into a place of perfect love and perfect faith. A person who is born of God is brought into an inward affection, a loyalty to the Lord Jesus that shrinks from anything impure. He who believes that Jesus is the Christ overcomes the world. It is a faith that works by love.

Just as we have heart fellowship with our Lord, our faith cannot be daunted. We cannot doubt in our hearts. There comes, as we go on with God, a wonderful association, an impartation of His Word, and we believe the promises He has so graciously given to us. We are made partakers of His very essence and life. The Lord is made to us a Bridegroom, and we are His bride. His words come to us, expelling what is natural and bringing what is divine.

Ever Increasing Faith

QUESTIONS TO CONSIDER
1. Do you really believe that all things are possible? Why or why not?
2. How can you destroy your doubts about Christ's ability to move mountains?

A PRAYERFUL RESPONSE
Lord, as I increase in love for You, please decrease my spiritual doubts. Amen.

PART TWO

RECEIVING THE POWER

When the Holy Spirit comes, He comes
to empower you to be an effective witness.
At one time a lady wrote and asked if I could come help her.
She said she was blind, having two blood clots behind her eyes.
When I reached the house they brought the blind woman to me.
We were together for some time and then the power of God fell.
Rushing to the window she exclaimed, "I can see! Oh, I can see!
The blood is gone, I can see."

She then inquired about receiving the Holy Spirit
and confessed that for ten years
she had been fighting our position.
She said, "I could not bear these tongues,
but God has settled the whole thing today.
I now want the baptism in the Holy Spirit."
The Lord graciously baptized her in the Spirit.

FAITH THAT PREVAILS

SMITH WIGGLESWORTH'S INSIGHT
God gives us His power so we can minister in His way.

PURGING THE OLD LIFE

THOUGHT FOR TODAY

The Holy Spirit fills people whom Christ has cleansed from sin.

WISDOM FROM SCRIPTURE

In the first book, *Theophilus*, I wrote about all that Jesus did and taught from the beginning until the day when he was taken up to heaven, after giving instructions through the Holy Spirit to the apostles whom he had chosen.

After his suffering he presented himself alive to them by many convincing proofs, appearing to them during forty days and speaking about the kingdom of God.

While staying with them, he ordered them not to leave Jerusalem, but to wait there for the promise of the Father. "This," he said, "is what you have heard from me; for John baptized with water, but you will be baptized with the Holy Spirit not many days from now."

So when they had come together, they asked him, "Lord, is this the time when you will restore the kingdom to Israel?"

He replied, "It is not for you to know the times or periods that the Father has set by his own authority. But you will receive power when the Holy Spirit has come upon you; and you will be my witnesses in Jerusalem, in all Judea and Samaria, and to the ends of the earth."

When he had said this, as they were watching, he was lifted up, and a cloud took him out of their sight.

While he was going and they were gazing up toward

heaven, suddenly two men in white robes stood by them.

They said, "Men of Galilee, why do you stand looking up toward heaven? This Jesus, who has been taken up from you into heaven, will come in the same way as you saw him go into heaven."

ACTS 1:1-11, NRSV

INSIGHTS FROM SMITH WIGGLESWORTH

The disciples had been asking whether the Lord would at that time restore the kingdom to Israel. Christ told them it was not for them to know the times and seasons the Father had put in His own power, but He promised them that when they received the Holy Spirit, they should receive power to witness for Him in all the world. To receive the Holy Spirit is to receive power with God and power with men.

There is a power which is of God and a power which is of Satan. When the Holy Spirit fell in the early days, a number of spiritists came to our meetings. They thought we had received something like they had and they were coming to have a good time. They filled the two front rows of our mission.

When the power of God fell, these imitators began shaking and muttering under the power of the devil. The Spirit of the Lord came mightily upon me and I cried, "Now, you devils, clear out of this!" And out they went. I followed them out into the street and then they turned around and cursed me. There was power from below but it was no match for the power of the Holy Spirit, and they soon had to retreat.

The Lord wants all saved people to receive power from on high—power to witness, power to act, power to live, and power to show forth the divine manifestation of God within. The power of God will take you out of your own plans and put you into the plan of God. You will be unmantled and divested of that which is purely yourself and put into a divine order. The Lord will change you and put His mind where yours was, and it will be God working in you and through you to do His own good pleasure through the power of the Spirit within.

Someone has said that you are no good until you have your "I" knocked out. Christ must reign within, and life in the Holy Spirit means at all times the subjection of your own will to make way for the working out of the good and acceptable and perfect will of God.

I was holding a meeting in London and at the close a man came to me and said, "We are not allowed to hold meetings in this hall after eleven o'clock, and we would like you to come home with us, I am so hungry for God." The wife said she, too, was hungry, so I agreed to go with them.

At about 12:30 we arrived at their house. The man began stirring up the fire and said, "Now we will have a good supper."

I said to them, "I did not come here for your warm fire, your supper, or your bed. I came here because I thought you were hungry to get more of God." We got down to pray and at about 3:30 the Lord baptized the wife, and she spoke in tongues as the Spirit gave utterance. At about 5:00 I spoke to the husband and asked how he was getting on.

He replied, "God has broken my iron, stubborn will." He had not received the baptism, but God had wrought a mighty work within him.

The following day at his business, everyone could tell a great change had come over him. Before, he had been a walking terror. The men who labored for him had looked upon him as a devil because of the way he acted; but coming into contact with the power of God that night completely changed him. Before this he had made a religious profession, but he had never truly entered into the experience of the new birth until that night when the power of God surged mightily through his home.

A short while afterward I went to this man's home, and his two sons ran to me and kissed me, saying, "We have a new father."

Previous to this, the boys had often said to their mother, "Mother, we cannot stand it at home any longer. We will have to leave." But the Lord changed the whole situation that night as we prayed together.

On my second visit the Lord baptized this man in the Holy Spirit. The Holy Spirit will reveal false positions, pull the mask off any refuge of lies, and clean up and remove all false conditions. When the Holy Spirit came in, that man's house and business were entirely changed.

The Holy Spirit will come when a person is cleansed. There must be a purging of the old life. I never saw anyone baptized who was not clean within.

Faith That Prevails

Questions to Consider

1. Do you know if you have been filled with God's Spirit? Why or why not?
2. What sin needs to be cleansed away so you can walk in the fullness of the Spirit?

A Prayerful Response

Lord, cleanse me of sin and purge out my old life so I can be filled with Your Spirit. Amen.

The Humility of Service

Thought for Today

When we fulfill humble tasks, God can deepen us spiritually.

Wisdom from Scripture

The word of God continued to spread; the number of the disciples increased greatly in Jerusalem, and a great many of the priests became obedient to the faith.

Stephen, full of grace and power, did great wonders and signs among the people.

Then some of those who belonged to the synagogue of the Freedmen (as it was called), Cyrenians, Alexandrians, and others of those from Cilicia and Asia, stood up and argued with Stephen.

But they could not withstand the wisdom and the Spirit with which he spoke.

Then they secretly instigated some men to say, "We have heard him speak blasphemous words against Moses and God."

They stirred up the people as well as the elders and the scribes; then they suddenly confronted him, seized him, and brought him before the council.

They set up false witnesses who said, "This man never stops saying things against this holy place and the law; for we have heard him say that this Jesus of Nazareth will destroy this place and will change the customs that Moses handed on to us."

And all who sat in the council looked intently at him, and they saw that his face was like the face of an angel.

ACTS 6:7-15, NRSV

INSIGHTS FROM SMITH WIGGLESWORTH

In the days when the number of disciples multiplied there developed a situation which caused the Twelve to make a definite decision not to occupy themselves with serving tables, but to give themselves continually to prayer and to the ministry of the Word. How important it is for all of God's ministers to be continually in prayer and feeding on the Scriptures of Truth.

The Twelve told the rest to find seven men to look after the business end of things. They were to be men of honest report and filled with the Holy Spirit. These were just ordinary men who were chosen, but they were filled with the Holy Spirit, and this infilling lifts a person to a plane above the ordinary. It does not take a cultured or learned person to fill a position in God's Church; what God requires is a yielded, consecrated, holy life. He can make of such a flame of fire. Baptized with the Holy Spirit and fire!

The multitude chose seven men to serve tables. They were doubtless faithful in their appointed tasks, but we see that God soon had a better choice for two of them. Philip was so full of the Holy Spirit that he could have a revival wherever God put him down. Men chose him to serve tables, but God chose him to win souls.

Oh, if I could only stir you up to see that as you are faithful in performing the humblest office, God can fill you with His Spirit and make you a chosen vessel for Himself, promoting you to a place of mighty ministry in the salvation of souls and healing of the sick. There is nothing impossible to someone filled with the Holy Spirit. It is beyond all human comprehension. When you are filled with the power of the Holy Spirit, God will work wonderfully wherever you go.

When you are filled with the Spirit you will know the voice of God. I want to give you one illustration of this. When I was on my way to Australia recently, our boat stopped at Aden and at Bombay. In the first place the people came round the ship selling their wares—beautiful carpets and all sorts of oriental things. There was one man selling some ostrich feathers. As I was looking over the side of the ship watching the trading, a gentleman said to me, "Would you go shares with me in buying that bunch of feathers?" What did I want with feathers? I had no use for such things and no room for them either. But the gentleman put the question to me again, "Will you go shares with me in buying that bunch?"

The Spirit of God said to me, "Do it."

The price of the feathers was three pounds, but the gentleman said, "I have no money with me, but if you will pay the man for them, I will send the cash down to you by the purser." I paid for the feathers and gave the gentleman his share.

I said to him, "No, please don't give that money to the purser. I want you to bring it personally to my cabin."

I said to the Lord, "What about these feathers?" He showed me that He had a purpose in my purchasing them.

At about ten o'clock the gentleman came to my cabin and said, "I've brought the money." I said to him, "It is not your money I want, it is your soul I am seeking for God." Right there he opened up the whole plan of his life and began to seek God, and that morning he wept his way through to salvation.

You have no idea what God can do through you when you are filled with His Spirit. Every day and every hour you can have the divine leading of God. To be filled with the Holy

Spirit means much in every way. I have seen some who have been suffering for years, and when they have been filled with the Holy Spirit all of their sickness has passed away. The Spirit of God has made real to them the life of Jesus, and they have been completely liberated of every sickness and infirmity.

Look at Stephen. He was just an ordinary man chosen to serve tables, but the Holy Spirit was in him. Stephen was full of faith and power and did great wonders and miracles among the people. There was no resisting the wisdom and the Spirit by which he spoke. How important it is that every person be filled with the Holy Spirit.

I want to impress the importance of this upon you. It is not healing I am presenting to you—it is the living Christ. It is a glorious fact that the Son of God came down to bring liberty to the captives.

Stephen was just an ordinary man clothed with the divine. He was full of faith and power, and great wonders and miracles were wrought by him. Oh, this life in the Holy Spirit! This life of deep, inward revelation, of transformation from one state to another, of growing in grace and in all knowledge and in the power of the Spirit, and of constant revelation of the might of His power. It is the only thing that will enable us to stand. *Ever Increasing Faith*

QUESTIONS TO CONSIDER
1. What humble service might God be asking of you?
2. What spiritual lesson can you learn through this humble task?

A PRAYERFUL RESPONSE
Lord, I will serve You humbly in the task set before me. Amen.

A Thirst for New Wine

Thought for Today

When we thirst for Jesus, He fills us with the new wine of the Holy Spirit.

Wisdom from Scripture

Do not fear, O soil; be glad and rejoice, for the LORD has done great things!

Do not fear, you animals of the field, for the pastures of the wilderness are green; the tree bears its fruit, the fig tree and vine give their full yield.

O children of Zion, be glad and rejoice in the LORD your God; for he has given the early rain for your vindication, he has poured down for you abundant rain, the early and the later rain, as before.

The threshing floors shall be full of grain, the vats shall overflow with wine and oil.

I will repay you for the years that the swarming locust has eaten, the hopper, the destroyer, and the cutter, my great army, which I sent against you.

You shall eat in plenty and be satisfied, and praise the name of the LORD your God, who has dealt wondrously with you. And my people shall never again be put to shame.

You shall know that I am in the midst of Israel, and that I, the LORD, am your God and there is no other. And my people shall never again be put to shame.

Then afterward I will pour out my spirit on all flesh; your sons and your daughters shall prophesy, your old men shall dream dreams, and your young men shall see visions.

JOEL 2:21-28, NRSV

It is a settled thing in heaven that the latter rain is greater than the former rain (Jl 2:28; Acts 2:16-21). Some of our hearts have been greatly moved by the former rain, but it is the latter rain we are crying for. What will it be like when the time comes and the heart of God is satisfied? We remember what happened on the day of Pentecost: "And [they] began to speak with other tongues, as the Spirit gave them utterance" (Acts 2:4).

What a lovely thought that the words they spoke were from the Holy Spirit! We are having to learn whether we like it or not that when we come to our end, God is only the beginning. Then it is all God, and the Lord Jesus stands forth in the midst with such divine glory that we are impelled, filled, led perfectly. Nothing else will meet the need of this world.

There is something beautiful about how the people in Jerusalem recognized that Peter and John had been with Jesus. There was something so real in these disciples, so much like their Master: "Now when they saw the boldness of Peter and John, and perceived that they were unlearned and ignorant men, they marveled; and they took knowledge of them, that they had been with Jesus" (Acts 4:13).

The outstanding thing in the life of Jesus, more than anything else, was the fact that people glorified God in Him. When God is glorified and gets the right of way and the minds of His people, the people are as He is: filled with God. Whatever it costs, it must be. Let it be so. Filled with God!

The only thing that helps people is to tell them the latest thing God has given us from the glory. There is nothing outside of salvation. We are filled, immersed, clothed; there must be nothing felt, seen, or spoken about but the mighty power of the Holy Spirit. We are new creatures in Christ Jesus, baptized in a new nature. "He that believeth on Me,… out of his belly shall flow rivers of living water" (Jn 7:38). The very life of the risen Christ in everything, moving us to do His will.

There is something we have not yet reached, but praise God for the thirst! For the thirst is of God; the plan and purpose is of God. God's plan, God's thought, God's vessel, and God's servant. We are in the world to meet the need, but not of the world or its spirit. Through God incarnate in humanity, we become partakers of the divine nature to manifest the life of Jesus to the world.

The world misunderstands, just as they did on the day of Pentecost: "Others mocking said, 'These men are full of new wine'" (Acts 2:13). That is what we want: new wine. A new order, a new inspiration, a new manifestation. A power all new as if you were born (as you are) into a new creation.

It has a freshness about it! It has a beauty about it! It will create in others the desire for the same taste as the three thousand felt, tasted, and enjoyed. Some looked on. Others drank with a new faith never seen before—a new manifestation, a new realization all divine, straight from heaven, from the throne of the glorified Lord. It is God's will to fill us with that wine, to make us ready to burst forth with new rivers of fresh energy.

What shall we do? Believe! Stretch out! Press on! Let there be a new entering in, a new passion to have it. We must be beside ourselves; we must drink deeply of the new wine so that multitudes may find satisfaction too.

The new wine is to have a new bottle—it needs a new vessel. If anything of the old life is left, not put to death and destroyed, there will be a rending and a breaking. The new wine and the old bottle will not work in harmony. It must be new wine and a new wineskin; then there will be nothing to drop off when Jesus comes.

When the Spirit is in control of our bodies, our bodies change until we will be like Him. "Who shall change our vile body, that it may be fashioned like unto His glorious body, according to the working whereby He is able even to subdue all things unto Himself" (Phil 3:21).

I desire you to be so filled with the Spirit, so hungry, so thirsty, that nothing will satisfy you but seeing Jesus. I hope you get thirstier every day, drier every day, until the floods come and the Master passes by.

Christ will minister to you and through you His life, His inspiration for a hurting world. His death on the cross was painful, but He accomplished the purpose for which He came. "It is finished," He cried (Jn 19:30).

Let the cry never stop until the heart of Jesus is satisfied, until the earth is filled with the knowledge of the glory of the Lord, as the waters cover the sea.

The Anointing of His Spirit

QUESTIONS TO CONSIDER
1. Why would God ask that we hunger and thirst for the Holy Spirit?
2. How can you deepen your passion for the Holy Spirit?

A PRAYERFUL RESPONSE
Lord, I hunger and thirst for Your new wine of the Spirit. Amen.

DAY 12

The Testing Road

Thought for Today
Each day we choose whether we will follow Jesus.

Wisdom from Scripture
Blessed be the God and Father of our Lord Jesus Christ, who has blessed us in Christ with every spiritual blessing in the heavenly places, just as he chose us in Christ before the foundation of the world to be holy and blameless before him in love.

He destined us for adoption as his children through Jesus Christ, according to the good pleasure of his will, to the praise of his glorious grace that he freely bestowed on us in the Beloved.

In him we have redemption through his blood, the forgiveness of our trespasses, according to the riches of his grace that he lavished on us. With all wisdom and insight he has made known to us the mystery of his will, according to his good pleasure that he set forth in Christ, as a plan for the fullness of time, to gather up all things in him, things in heaven and things on earth.

In Christ we have also obtained an inheritance, having been destined according to the purpose of him who accomplishes all things according to his counsel and will, so that we, who were the first to set our hope on Christ, might live for the praise of his glory.

EPHESIANS 1:3-12, NRSV

Scripture tells us that the delaying of the promise and the testing of Abraham was the seed of future generations who believed in God. "And being fully persuaded that what He had promised, He was able also to perform" (Rom 4:21). Therefore, it was imputed unto Abraham for righteousness, and not to him only, but to you and everyone else who believes.

Have you ever been tested? It is the greatest thing in the world to be tested. You never know what you are made of until you are tested. Some people say, "Oh, I don't know why my lot is such a heavy one," and God puts them into the fire again. He knows how much to do it, I can tell you—He is a blessed God. There is no such thing as a groan when God gets hold of you. When we really get in the will of God, He can make our enemies to be at peace with us. It is wonderful.

Listen to these words and take them into your being, for they will keep you during testing times: "There hath no temptation taken you but such as is common to man: but God is faithful, who will not suffer you to be tempted above that ye are able; but will with the temptation also make a way to escape, that ye may be able to bear it" (1 Cor 10:13).

I was taken to see a young woman who was very ill. The young man who showed me the way said, "I am afraid we shall not be able to do much here because of her mother, and the doctors are coming."

"This is the reason God brought me here," I said. When I prayed, the young woman was instantly healed by the power of God. After that crowds came, and I ministered to the sick among them for two hours. God the Holy Spirit tells us in our hearts that it is only He who can do it.

The secret for the future is living and moving in the power

of the Holy Spirit. One thing I rejoice in is that there need not be an hour or moment when we do not know that the Holy Spirit is upon us.

Oh, this glorious life in God is beyond expression. It is God manifest in the flesh. Oh, this glorious unction of the Holy Spirit—that we move by the Spirit. He should be our continual life. The inward person receives the Holy Spirit instantly with great joy and blessedness. He cannot express it. Then the power of the Spirit, this breath of God, takes the things of Jesus and sends forth as a river the utterances of the Spirit.

The Holy Spirit has the last thoughts on things that God wants to give. Glory to God for the Holy Spirit! We must make sure to live in the place where we say, "What wilt Thou have me to do?" and where He can work in us "to will and to do of His good pleasure" (Eph 1:9).

I believe there is a day coming that you have not yet conceived. This is the testing road. This is the place where your whole body has to be covered with the wings of God. This is the thing for which God is getting you ready, the most wonderful thing your heart can conceive.

How can you get into it? First of all, have you continued with the Lord in His temptations? He had been in trials; He had been in temptation. There is not one of us that is tempted beyond what He was.

If we can be tried, if we can be tempted on any line, Jesus speaks to us as well as His faithful disciples: "Ye are they which have continued with me in my temptations" (Lk 22:28). Have faith and God will keep you pure in the temptation.

How shall we reach it? In Matthew 19:28 Jesus said, "Ye which have followed Me in the regeneration when the Son of man shall sit on the throne of his glory, ye also shall sit upon twelve thrones, judging the twelve tribes of Israel."

Every day is a regeneration, a day of advancement, a place of choice. Every day you find yourself in need of fresh consecration. If you are in a place to yield, God moves you to the place of regeneration. *Only Believe!*

QUESTIONS TO CONSIDER

1. What does it mean for you to continue with Jesus in His temptations?
2. How do you need to yield and consecrate your life to God today?

A PRAYERFUL RESPONSE

Lord, I want to continue with You in Your temptations. Give me the strength of Your Spirit. Amen.

The Place of Power

Thought for Today

In spiritually dry places, God can fill us with His Spirit's power.

Wisdom from Scripture

Jesus, full of the Holy Spirit, returned from the Jordan and was led by the Spirit in the wilderness, where for forty days he was tempted by the devil. He ate nothing at all during those days, and when they were over, he was famished.

The devil said to him, "If you are the Son of God, command this stone to become a loaf of bread."

Jesus answered him, "It is written, 'One does not live by bread alone.'"

Then the devil led him up and showed him in an instant all the kingdoms of the world.

And the devil said to him, "To you I will give their glory and all this authority; for it has been given over to me, and I give it to anyone I please. If you, then, will worship me, it will all be yours."

Jesus answered him, "It is written, 'Worship the Lord your God, and serve only him.'"

Then the devil took him to Jerusalem, and placed him on the pinnacle of the temple, saying to him, "If you are the Son of God, throw yourself down from here, for it is written, 'He will command his angels concerning you, to protect you, and on their hands they will bear you up, so that you will not dash your foot against a stone.'"

Jesus answered him, "It is said, 'Do not put the Lord your God to the test.'"

Luke 4:1-12, NRSV

The Holy Spirit took Jesus away into the wilderness, with its darkness and deprivation. For forty days He was without food, but because of the presence and the power of the Holy Spirit within and on Him, Jesus was certain of victory. With this power He faced the wild beasts of the wilderness and the deprivation of every human sustenance.

And then at the end of forty days, in that holy attainment, Jesus was forced into such persecution and trial that probably has never attacked a person before. And in that place God sustained Him mightily.

With what? With this holy, blessed anointing which was upon Him. This power from on high brings prophecy to bear upon Satan so that Jesus has a sword with which He can defeat and almost slay Satan every time by reminding him, "It is written" (Lk 4:4).

In the fourteenth verse we see the result of this wilderness victory: "Jesus returned in the power of the Spirit into Galilee: and there went out a fame of him through all the region round about. And he taught in their synagogues, being glorified of all" (verses 14-15). After the trials, after all the temptations and everything, Jesus came out more full of God, more clothed in the Spirit, more ready for the fight. The endowment with power had such an effect upon Him that other people saw it and flocked to hear Him, and great blessings came to the land.

God in like manner wants to give us victory. What does the Word say? "Be still, and know that I am God" (Ps 46:10). Be in the place of tranquillity where we know He is controlling and moving us by the mighty power of His Spirit.

Beloved, that is a place we can reach. Truly God wants to begin this in us. We must always remember that it is God who is the Creator, and His creative power is available at this moment. He knows where there is barrenness and where there is thirsty land, and it is He who can bring forth springs of water.

There are many dry places. Indeed, nearly every town I go to is said to be the driest of places—"the hardest town in the kingdom," they will say. And yet the Lord's hand is not shortened that it cannot save (see Is 59:1). It is in humanity's extremity that God finds His opportunity, and He can awaken even you.

And so God wants us to cheer up. But if we are to do the will of God at the right time and place, we must yield to the Spirit and obey Him so as to give God a fair chance.

I want to point out something about John the Divine whose preaching got him into trouble. He preached all over the country, and the enemies of Christ gnashed upon him with their teeth, and they tried to the best of their power to destroy him. Tradition says they even put John into a pot of boiling oil, but like a cat he seemed to have nine lives.

I tell you there is something in the power of the Holy Spirit. When God wants to keep a person, nothing can destroy him. Our lives are in the hands of God. What can separate us from the love of God? Can heights or depths? Is there anything that can separate us? No, praise God! Nothing can separate us.

John's enemies found they could not kill him, so they cast him away on the rocky and desolate island of Patmos. They thought that would be the end of him. And there, on that lonely isle, he was "in the Spirit" (Rv 1:10). Have you ever been there? The very place that was not fit for humanity was the place where John was most filled with God, and where he was most ready for the revelation of Jesus.

Oh, beloved, I tell you there is something in the baptism

in the Holy Spirit worthy of our whole attention, worthy of our whole consideration in every way. The baptism in the Holy Spirit! Yes, the barren wilderness, the rocky and desolate isle, the dry land, and the most unfriendly place may be filled with God.

John was in the Spirit on the Lord's Day, and behind him he heard "a great voice, as of a trumpet" (Rv 1:10). Immediately he received a revelation, which one cannot read without being blessed. The revelation given to John contained a series of holy truths that have yet to be fulfilled, but they will be fulfilled to the letter. We read wonderful things there.

Blessed be God, we can come to that place John speaks about. Jesus can reveal His mind to us from time to time. If you only stop to think about it, you will see you are in a position a thousand times better than John's. In that barren place he was filled with the Spirit. You have no excuse, for the lines have fallen to you in pleasant places.

John was in such a blessed condition of fellowship with God that immediately he was in the Spirit. Immediately! It means that God wants us to be in a place where the least breath of heaven makes us all on fire, ready for everything.

You say, "How can I have that?" Oh, you can have that as easy as anything.

"Can I?" Yes, it is simple as well as possible.

"How?" Let heaven come in, let the Holy Spirit take possession of you, and when He comes into your body you will find that is the keynote of the spirit of joy and the spirit of rapture.

If you will allow the Holy Spirit to have full control, you will find you are living in the Spirit. You will discover that your opportunities will be God's opportunities. And you will find that you have come to the right place at the right time.

The Anointing of His Spirit

Questions to Consider
1. What does it feel like to be in a dry place? Are you in a spiritually dry place now?
2. How can you be in God's right place at the right time?

A Prayerful Response
Lord, in a dry place, fill me with Your mighty and rejuvenating power. Amen.

NEVER LOOK BACK

THOUGHT FOR TODAY

Life in the Spirit requires that we not look back at our old life.

WISDOM FROM SCRIPTURE

And so, brothers and sisters, I could not speak to you as spiritual people, but rather as people of the flesh, as infants in Christ.

I fed you with milk, not solid food, for you were not ready for solid food. Even now you are still not ready, for you are still of the flesh. For as long as there is jealousy and quarreling among you, are you not of the flesh, and behaving according to human inclinations?

For when one says, "I belong to Paul," and another, "I belong to Apollos," are you not merely human?

What then is Apollos? What is Paul? Servants through whom you came to believe, as the Lord assigned to each.

I planted, Apollos watered, but God gave the growth.

So neither the one who plants nor the one who waters is anything, but only God who gives the growth.

The one who plants and the one who waters have a common purpose, and each will receive wages according to the labor of each.

For we are God's servants, working together; you are God's field, God's building.

According to the grace of God given to me, like a skilled master builder I laid a foundation, and someone else is building on it. Each builder must choose with care how to build on it.

> For no one can lay any foundation other than the one that has been laid; that foundation is Jesus Christ.
>
> 1 CORINTHIANS 3:1-11, NRSV

INSIGHTS FROM SMITH WIGGLESWORTH

We are told that we are to leave the first principles of the doctrine of Christ and go on to perfection, not laying again the foundation of repentance from dead works and the doctrine of baptisms and other first principles (see Hebrews 6). What would you think of a builder who was everlastingly pulling down his house and putting in fresh foundations?

Never look back if you want the power of God in your life. You will find out that in the measure you have allowed yourself to look back you have missed what God has for you. The Holy Spirit shows us that we must never look back to the law of sin and death from which we have been delivered. God has brought us into a new order of things, a life of love and liberty in Christ Jesus that is beyond all human comprehension.

Many are brought into this new life through the power of the Spirit of God and then, like the Galatians, who ran well at the beginning, they try to perfect themselves on the lines of legalism. They go back from the life in the Spirit to a life on natural lines. God is not pleased with this, for He has no place for the person who has lost the vision.

The only thing to do is repent. Don't try to cover up anything. If you have been tripped up in any way, confess it, and then look to God to bring you to a place of stability of faith where your whole walk will be in the Spirit.

We all ought to have a clear conviction that salvation is of the Lord. It is more than a human order of things. If the enemy can move you from a place of faith, he can get you outside the plan of God. The moment a man falls into sin, divine life ceases to flow, and his life becomes one of helplessness.

But this is not God's will for any of His children. Stand on the knowledge that you are a child of God; remember that as your hope is set in Christ, it should have a purifying effect on your life.

There is life and power in the seed of the Word that is implanted within. There is more power in that Word of His than in any human objections. God's will for every one of us is that we shall reign in life by Jesus Christ. We must come to see how wonderful we are in God and how helpless we are in ourselves.

God declared Himself more mighty than every opposing power when He cast out the power of darkness from heaven. The same power that cast Satan out of heaven dwells in everyone who is born of God. If you would but realize this, you would reign in life.

When you see people bound by an evil power, when you see the powers of evil manifesting themselves, always put the question, "Did Jesus come in the flesh?" I have never seen an evil power answer in the affirmative. God means for you to be in a place of overcoming. He has put a Force within you whereby you may defeat the devil.

In this new life in the Spirit, in this New Covenant life, we will love the things that are right and pure and holy, and shudder at all things that are wrong. Jesus was able to say, "The prince of this world cometh, and hath nothing in me" (Jn 14:30). The moment we are filled with the Spirit of God we are brought into a wonderful condition, and as we continue to be filled with the Spirit, the enemy cannot have an inch of territory in us.

Do you believe that you can be so filled with the Spirit that a man who is not living right can be judged and convicted by your presence? As we go on in the life of the Spirit it will be said of us, "in whose eyes a vile person is condemned" (Ps 15:4). Jesus moved in this realm, and His life was a constant reproof to the wickedness around Him. God through Him has brought us into the place of sonship, and I believe that the Holy Spirit can make something of us and bring us to the same place.

All that we do must be done under the anointing of the Spirit. The trouble is that we have been living under the law. We must believe what the Holy Spirit says through Paul—that all this ministration of condemnation that has hindered our liberty in Christ is done away. As far as we are concerned, all that old order of things is forever done away, and the Spirit of God has brought in a new life of purity and love.

The Holy Spirit takes it for granted that we are finished with all the things of the old life when we become new in Christ. In the life in the Spirit, the old allurements have lost their power. The devil will meet us at every turn, but the Spirit of God will always lift up a standard against him.

There is a continual transformation in this life. As we behold the Lord and His glory we are changed into the same image from glory to glory, even by the Spirit of the Lord. There is a continual unveiling, a constant revelation, a repeated clothing from above. I want you to promise God never to look back, never to go back to what the Spirit has said, is "done away."   *Ever Increasing Faith*

QUESTIONS TO CONSIDER

1. Are there things that tempt you to look back at your old life? If so, what are they?
2. How can you keep looking forward and following Jesus?

A Prayerful Response

Lord, I will not look back at my old life, but will look forward to spiritual maturity. Amen.

THE ORDINARY MADE EXTRAORDINARY

THOUGHT FOR TODAY

The Holy Spirit turns ordinary people into extraordinary believers.

WISDOM FROM SCRIPTURE

While he was still speaking, some people came from the leader's house to say, "Your daughter is dead. Why trouble the teacher any further?"

But overhearing what they said, Jesus said to the leader of the synagogue, "Do not fear, only believe."

He allowed no one to follow him except Peter, James, and John, the brother of James.

When they came to the house of the leader of the synagogue, he saw a commotion, people weeping and wailing loudly.

When he had entered, he said to them, "Why do you make a commotion and weep? The child is not dead but sleeping."

And they laughed at him. Then he put them all outside, and took the child's father and mother and those who were with him, and went in where the child was.

He took her by the hand and said to her, "Talitha cum," which means, "Little girl, get up!"

And immediately the girl got up and began to walk about (she was twelve years of age). At this they were overcome with amazement.

MARK 5:35-42, NRSV

I love to sing that wonderful chorus, "Only Believe," because it is scriptural. It is from the words of Jesus to the synagogue ruler whose daughter had died (see Mk 5:36). The chorus says:

> Only believe! Only believe!
> All things are possible,
> Only believe!
> Only believe! Only believe!
> All things are possible,
> Only believe!

Our Lord Jesus says, "Only believe." He has ordained complete victory over every difficulty, over every power of evil, over every depravity. Every sin is covered by Calvary.

Our Lord Jesus says, "All power is given unto me in heaven and in earth" (Mt 28:18). He longs that we should be filled with faith and with the Holy Spirit, and declares to us, "He that believeth on me, the works that I do shall he do also; and greater works than these shall he do; because I go unto my Father" (Jn 14:12).

Jesus has gone to the Father. He sits in the place of power and He exercises His power not only in heaven, but on earth, for He has all power on earth as well as in heaven. Hallelujah! What an open door to us if we will but believe Him.

The disciples were men after the flesh just like us. God sent them forth, joined to the Lord and identified with Him. Peter, John, and Thomas—how different they were! Impulsive Peter, ever ready to go forth without a stop. John, the beloved, leaning on the Master's breast. Thomas, with hard nature and defiant spirit, exclaimed, "Except I shall see in his hands the print of the nails, and put my finger into the print of the nails, and thrust my hand into his side, I will not believe" (Jn 20:25b).

What strange flesh! How peculiar! But the Master could mold them. There was no touch like His. Under His touch even stonyhearted Thomas believed.

Ah, my God, how You have had to manage some of us. Have we not been strange and very peculiar? But when Your hand comes upon us, You can speak to us in such a way—a word, a look, and we are broken.

God sees our bitter tears and our weeping night after night. There is none like Him. He knows. He forgives. We cannot forgive ourselves. We oftentimes would give the world to forget, but we cannot. The devil won't let us forget. But God has forgiven and forgotten.

Do you believe self, or the devil, or God? Which are you going to believe?

Believe God. The past is under the blood and God has forgiven and forgotten, for when He forgives, He forgets. Praise the Lord! Hallelujah! We are baptized to believe and receive.

You may be ordinary, but God wants to make you extraordinary in the Holy Spirit. God is ready to touch and transform you right now.

Once a woman stood in a meeting asking for prayer. I prayed for her and she was healed. She cried out, "It is a miracle! It is a miracle! It is a miracle!" That is what God wants to do for us all the time. As soon as we get free in the Holy Spirit, something will happen. Let us pursue the best things and let God have His right of way.

It is God's intention to make you a new creation, with all the old things passed away and all things within you truly of God; to bring in a new, divine order, a perfect love, and an unlimited faith. Will you have it? Redemption is free. Arise in the activity of faith and God will heal you as you rise. Only believe and receive in faith. May God bless to you this word and fill you full of His Holy Spirit.

The Spirit of God will always reveal the Lord Jesus Christ. Serve Him, love Him, be filled with Him. It is lovely to hear Him as He makes Himself known. Jesus is the same yesterday, today, and forever. He is willing to fill you with the Holy Spirit and faith.   *The Anointing of His Spirit*

QUESTIONS TO CONSIDER
1. In what ways do you feel like an ordinary person?
2. In what ways would you like God to make you extra-ordinary?

A PRAYERFUL RESPONSE
Lord, please fill my ordinary self with Your extraordinary power. Amen.

DAY 16

CONCERNING SPIRITUAL GIFTS

THOUGHT FOR TODAY

Being filled with the Spirit is more important than exercising spiritual gifts.

WISDOM FROM SCRIPTURE

Now concerning spiritual gifts, brothers and sisters, I do not want you to be uninformed.

You know that when you were pagans, you were enticed and led astray to idols that could not speak.

Therefore I want you to understand that no one speaking by the Spirit of God ever says "Let Jesus be cursed!" and no one can say "Jesus is Lord" except by the Holy Spirit.

Now there are varieties of gifts, but the same Spirit; and there are varieties of services, but the same Lord; and there are varieties of activities, but it is the same God who activates all of them in everyone.

To each is given the manifestation of the Spirit for the common good.

To one is given through the Spirit the utterance of wisdom, and to another the utterance of knowledge according to the same Spirit, to another faith by the same Spirit, to another gifts of healing by the one Spirit, to another the working of miracles, to another prophecy, to another the discernment of spirits, to another various kinds of tongues, to another the interpretation of tongues.

All these are activated by one and the same Spirit, who allots to each one individually just as the Spirit chooses.

For just as the body is one and has many members, and

all the members of the body, though many, are one body, so it is with Christ.

1 CORINTHIANS 12:1-12, NRSV

INSIGHTS FROM SMITH WIGGLESWORTH

There is a great weakness in the Church of Christ because of ignorance concerning the Spirit of God and His gifts. God would have us know His will concerning the power and manifestation of His Spirit. He would have us ever hungry to receive more of His Spirit.

Now there are diversities of gifts, but the same Spirit (1 Cor 12:4). Every manifestation of the Spirit is given that we might profit. When the Holy Spirit is moving in an assembly and His gifts are in operation, everyone will profit.

I have seen some who have been terribly switched. They believe in gifts, in prophecy, and they use these gifts apart from the power of the Holy Spirit. We must look to the Holy Spirit to show us the use of the gifts, what they are for, and when to use them, so that we may never use them without His power. I do not know of anything so tragic as people using a gift without the power. God save us from doing it.

A person who is filled with the Holy Spirit, while he may not be conscious of having any gift of the Spirit, can have the gifts made manifest to him. I have gone to many places to help and have found that under the unction of the Holy Spirit wonderful things have happened when the glory of the Lord was upon the people. Any person who is filled with God and filled with His Spirit might at any moment have any of the nine gifts made manifest through him without knowing he has a gift.

Sometimes I have wondered whether it was better to be always full of the Holy Spirit and to see signs and wonders and miracles without any consciousness of possessing a gift or whether it was better to know one has a gift. If you have received the gifts of the Spirit and they have been blessed, you should not use them without the power of God upon you. Some have used the prophetic gift without the holy touch and they have come into the realm of the natural; it has brought ruin, caused dissatisfaction, broken hearts, and upset assemblies. Do not seek the gifts unless you are purposed to abide in the Holy Spirit.

While it is right to covet earnestly the best gifts, you must recognize that the all-important thing is to be filled with the power of the Holy Spirit. You will never have trouble with people who are filled with the power of the Holy Spirit, but you will have a lot of trouble with people who have the gifts and have no power. The Lord wants us to be so filled with the Holy Spirit that it will be the Holy Spirit manifesting Himself through the gifts.

Where the glory of God alone is desired we can look for every needed gift to be made manifest. To glorify God is better than to idolize gifts. We prefer the Spirit of God to any gift; but we look for the Trinity in manifestation, different gifts by the same Spirit, different administrations but the same Lord, diversities of operation but the same God working all in all (see 1 Cor 12:4-6). Can you conceive of what it will mean for our triune God to be manifesting Himself in His fullness in our assemblies?

It is wonderful to be filled with the power of the Holy Spirit and for Him to serve His purposes through us. Through our lips divine utterances flow, our hearts rejoice, and our tongue is glad. An inward power is manifested in outward expression. Jesus Christ is glorified. As your faith in

Him is quickened, from within you there will flow rivers of living water. The Holy Spirit will pour through you like a great river of life, and thousands will be blessed because you are a yielded channel through whom the Spirit may flow.

The most important thing, the one thing that counts, is to see that we are filled with the Holy Spirit, filled to overflowing. Anything less than this is displeasing to God. We are commanded by God to be filled with the Spirit, and in the measure we fail in this we are that far short of the plan of God. The Lord would have us moving on from faith to faith, from glory to glory, from fullness to overflowing.

It is not good for us to be thinking in the past tense, but we should be moving on to the place where we dare to believe God. He has declared that after the Holy Spirit is come upon us we shall have power. I believe there is an avalanche of power from God to be apprehended if we will but catch the vision.

I desire to emphasize the importance of the Spirit's ministration and of the manifestation of the Spirit which is given to every person to profit. As you yield to the Spirit of the Lord He has power over your intellect, over your heart, and over your voice. The Holy Spirit has power to unveil Christ and to project the vision of Christ upon the canvas of your mind, and then He uses your tongue to glorify and magnify Him in a way that you could never do apart from the Spirit's power.

When a person is filled with the Spirit, he has no conception of what he has. We are so limited in our conception of what we have received. The only way we can know the power that has been given is through the ministration and manifestation of the Spirit of God. The nearer we get to God, the more conscious we are of the poverty of the human, and we cry with Isaiah, "I am undone, I am unclean" (Is 6:5). But

86

the Lord will bring the precious blood and the flaming coals for cleansing and refining and send us out to labor for Him, empowered by His Spirit.

Ever Increasing Faith

QUESTIONS TO CONSIDER

1. Are you aware of the spiritual gifts given to you? If so, what are they?
2. How can you keep these gifts from becoming more important than following Christ?

A PRAYERFUL RESPONSE

Lord, keep my eyes focused on Your Spirit rather than on Your gifts. Amen.

PART THREE

SOWING IN RIGHTEOUSNESS

At one time I was in a meeting in Ireland.

There were many sick carried to that meeting. There were many in
that place who were seeking the baptism of the Holy Spirit.

Some of them had been seeking for years.

There were sinners who were under mighty conviction.

There came a moment when the breath of God swept through
the meeting.

In about ten minutes every sinner was saved.

Everyone who had been seeking the Holy Spirit was baptized,
and every sick one was healed.

God is a reality and His power can never fail.

As our faith reaches out, God will meet us and the same rain
will fall.

It is the same blood that cleanseth, the same power,
the same Holy Spirit, and the same Jesus made real
through the power of the Holy Spirit!

What would happen if we should believe God?

EVER INCREASING FAITH

SMITH WIGGLESWORTH'S INSIGHT

When we sow in righteousness, we will reap in joy and
power.

89

LOVING RIGHTEOUSNESS

THOUGHT FOR TODAY

Righteousness opens the door to God's blessings.

WISDOM FROM SCRIPTURE

"You have loved righteousness and hated wickedness; therefore God, your God, has set you above your companions by anointing you with the oil of joy."

He also says, "In the beginning, O Lord, you laid the foundations of the earth, and the heavens are the work of your hands. They will perish, but you remain; they will all wear out like a garment. You will roll them up like a robe; like a garment they will be changed. But you remain the same, and your years will never end."

To which of the angels did God ever say, "Sit at my right hand until I make your enemies a footstool for your feet"?

Are not all angels ministering spirits sent to serve those who will inherit salvation?

We must pay more careful attention, therefore, to what we have heard, so that we do not drift away.

For if the message spoken by angels was binding, and every violation and disobedience received its just punishment, how shall we escape if we ignore such a great salvation? This salvation, which was first announced by the Lord, was confirmed to us by those who heard him.

HEBREWS 1:9-2:3, NIV

INSIGHTS FROM SMITH WIGGLESWORTH

It is the purpose of God that as we are indwelt by the Spirit of His Son, we should love righteousness and hate

91

iniquity. There is a place for us in Christ Jesus where we are no longer under condemnation but where the heavens are always open to us. God has a realm of divine life opening up to us where there are boundless possibilities, limitless power, untold resources, and victory over the power of the devil. I believe that as we are filled with the desire to press on into this life of true holiness, desiring only the glory of God, nothing can hinder our advancement.

Abraham attained to the place where he became a friend of God, on no other line than that of believing God. He believed God, and God counted that to him for righteousness. Righteousness was imputed to him for righteousness, on no other ground than that he believed God.

Can this be true of anybody else? Yes, every person in the world who is saved by faith is blessed along with faithful Abraham. The promise that came to Abraham because he believed God was that in him all the families of the earth should be blessed. When we believe God, there is no knowing where the blessing of our faith will end. You can hear him saying to Sarah, "There is no life in you and there is nothing in me, but God has promised us a son and I believe God." That kind of faith is a joy to our Father in heaven.

One day I was having a meeting and a young woman came to be healed of a goiter. Before she came she said to her mother, "I am going to be healed of this goiter." After one meeting she came forward and was prayed for. At the next meeting she got up and testified that she had been healed and added, "I shall be so happy to go and tell Mother that I have been wonderfully healed."

The next year when we were having the convention she came again. To the natural view it looked as though the goiter was just as big as ever; but that young woman was believing God and giving her testimony, saying, "I was here last year and the Lord wonderfully healed me. I want to tell you that this has been the best year of my life." She seemed to be greatly blessed in that meeting, and she went home to testify more strongly than ever that the Lord had healed her. She believed God.

The third year she was at the meeting again, and some people who looked at her exclaimed, "How big that goiter has become!" But when the testimony time came she was on her feet and testified, "Two years ago the Lord graciously healed me of goiter. Oh, I had a most wonderful healing. It is grand to be healed by the power of God."

That day someone said to her, "People will think there is something the matter with you. Why don't you look in the mirror? You will see your goiter is bigger than ever." That good woman went to the Lord about it and said, "Lord, You so wonderfully healed me two years ago. Won't You show all the people that You healed me?" She went to sleep peacefully that night, still believing God. The next day there was not a trace of that goiter.

You will note as you read 2 Peter 1:1-2 that grace and peace are multiplied through the knowledge of God; but first our faith comes through the righteousness of God. Note that righteousness comes first and knowledge afterward. It cannot be otherwise. If you expect any revelation of God apart from holiness, you will have only a mixture. Holiness opens the door to all the treasures of God. He must first bring us to the place where, like our Lord, we love righteousness and hate iniquity. Then He opens up to us these good treasures.

When we regard iniquity in our hearts, the Lord will not hear us; and it is only as we are made righteous and pure and holy through the precious blood of God's Son that we can enter into this life of holiness and righteousness. It is the righteousness of our Lord made real in us as our faith is stayed in Him.

After I was baptized with the Holy Spirit the Lord gave me a blessed revelation. I saw Adam and Eve turned out of the Garden for their disobedience and unable to partake of the tree of life, for the cherubim with flaming sword kept them away from the tree. When I was baptized I saw that I had begun to eat of this tree of life, and I saw the flaming sword round about. It was there to keep the devil away.

Oh, what privileges are ours when we are born of God! How marvelously He keeps us so the wicked one does not touch us. I see a place where Satan dares not come. Hidden in God. And He invites us all to share this wonderful place where our lives are hid with Christ in God, where we dwell in the secret place of the Most High and abide under the shadow of the Almighty. God has a place for you in that blessed realm of grace.

Peter goes on to say, "According as his divine power hath given unto us all things that pertain unto life and godliness, through the knowledge of him that hath called us to glory and virtue" (2 Pt 1:3). God is calling us to this realm of glory and virtue where, as we feed on His exceeding great and precious promises, we are made partakers of the divine nature. It is nothing less than the life of the Lord Himself imparted and flowing into our whole beings, so that our very body is quickened, so that every tissue and every drop of blood and our bones and joints and marrow receive this divine life.

God wants to establish our faith so we lay hold of this life, this divine nature of the Son of God, that our spirit, soul, and body will be sanctified wholly and preserved unto the coming of the Lord Jesus Christ. *Ever Increasing Faith*

QUESTIONS TO CONSIDER
1. How could righteous living increase your faith?
2. Have your soul and body received God's divine life? How do you know?

A PRAYERFUL RESPONSE
Lord, as You did with Abraham, please count my faith as righteousness. Amen.

THAT I MAY KNOW HIM

THOUGHT FOR TODAY

To know and identify with Christ is to die to ourselves.

WISDOM FROM SCRIPTURE

For it is we who are the circumcision, we who worship by the Spirit of God, who glory in Christ Jesus, and who put no confidence in the flesh—though I myself have reasons for such confidence.

If anyone else thinks he has reasons to put confidence in the flesh, I have more: circumcised on the eighth day, of the people of Israel, of the tribe of Benjamin, a Hebrew of Hebrews; in regard to the law, a Pharisee; as for zeal, persecuting the church; as for legalistic righteousness, faultless.

But whatever was to my profit I now consider loss for the sake of Christ. What is more, I consider everything a loss compared to the surpassing greatness of knowing Christ Jesus my Lord, for whose sake I have lost all things. I consider them rubbish, that I may gain Christ and be found in him, not having a righteousness of my own that comes from the law, but that which is through faith in Christ—the righteousness that comes from God and is by faith. I want to know Christ and the power of his resurrection and the fellowship of sharing in his sufferings, becoming like him in his death, and so, somehow, to attain to the resurrection from the dead.

Not that I have already obtained all this, or have already been made perfect, but I press on to take hold of that for which Christ Jesus took hold of me. Brothers, I do not consider myself yet to have taken hold of it. But one thing I do: Forgetting what is behind and straining toward what is ahead, I press on toward the goal to win the prize for which God has called me heavenward in Christ Jesus.

PHILIPPIANS 3:3-14, NIV

INSIGHTS FROM SMITH WIGGLESWORTH

Every day there must be a revival in our hearts. Every day must change us after God's fashion. We are to be made new all the time. There is no such thing as having all grace and knowledge. There is a beginning, and God would have us begin in power and never cease, but rise and go on to perfection.

Let us look at what God wants us to reach this day. "But what things were gained to me, those I counted as lost for Christ. Yea doubtless, and I count all things but loss for the excellency of the knowledge of Christ Jesus my Lord: for whom I have suffered the loss of all things, and do count them but dung, that I may win Christ" (Phil 3:7-8). Also we turn to Hebrews 10:32: "But call to remembrance the former days, in which, after ye were illuminated, ye endured a great fight of afflictions." I am positive that no one can attain likemindedness on these lines except by the illumination of the Spirit.

As Paul saw the depths and heights of the grandeur of God, he longed that he might win Him. Before his conversion, in his passion and zeal, Paul would do anything to bring Christians to death; that passion raged like a mighty lion. As he was going to Damascus, he heard the voice of Jesus saying, "Saul, Saul, why persecutest thou me?" (Acts 9:4). What broke him was the tenderness of God.

Beloved, it is always God's tenderness over our weakness and depravity that breaks us as well. If somebody came along

97

to thwart us, we would stand in our corner, but when we come to One who forgives us all, we know not what to do. Oh, to win Him!

There are a thousand things in the nucleus of a human heart which need softening every day. There are things in us that, unless God shows us the excellency of the knowledge of Him, will never be broken and brought to ashes. But God will do it. We are not merely to be saved, but to be saved a thousand times over! Oh, this transforming regeneration by the power of the Spirit of the living God makes me see there is a place to win Him, that I may stand complete in that place. As Jesus was, so am I to be. The Scriptures declare it; it shall be.

"And be found in him, not having mine own righteousness, which is of the law, but that which is through the faith of Christ, the righteousness which is of God by faith" (Phil 3:9). Not depending upon my works, but upon the faithfulness of God, being able under all circumstances to be hidden in Him, covered by the almighty presence of God!

Oh, but I must be found in Him! There is a place of seclusion, a place of rest and faith in Jesus where nothing else compares. Jesus came to His disciples on the water and they were terrified, but He said, "It is I; be not afraid" (Mt 14:27). He is always there. He is there in the storms as well as in the peace; He is there in the adversity. When shall we know He is there? When we are "found in Him," not having our own work, our own plan, but resting in the omnipotent plan of God.

Is there anything more? Oh, yes, we must see the next thing. Jesus taught that "except a corn of wheat fall into the ground and die, it abideth alone: but if it die, it bringeth forth much fruit" (Jn 12:24). God wants you to see that unless you are dead indeed, unless you come to a crucifixion, unless you die with Jesus, you are not in the fellowship of His sufferings.

May God move upon us in this life to bring us into an absolute death—not merely talking about it, not assuming it, but really dying to ourselves so God's life may indeed be made manifest. Paul said, "I count not myself to have apprehended: but this one thing I do, forgetting those things which are behind, and reaching forth unto those things which are before, I press toward the mark for the prize of the high calling of God in Christ Jesus" (Phil 3:13-14).

Paul had just said he was following after that for which he had been taken captive by Christ Jesus. I believe God wants us to be of the same mind, that we too may be able to say, "I know I have died." The Lord wants us to understand that we must come to a place where our natural life ceases, and by the power of God we rise into a life where God rules and reigns.

Do you long to know Him? Do you long to be found in Him? Your longing shall be satisfied today. This is the day of putting on and being clothed in God. Fall in the presence of God. Yield to His mighty power and obey the Spirit.

The Anointing of His Spirit

Questions to Consider

1. In what ways have you known the fellowship of Christ's sufferings?
2. How can you yield to the Holy Spirit today?

A Prayerful Response

Lord, teach me the fellowship and joy of Your sufferings. Amen.

LIVING EPISTLES OF CHRIST

THOUGHT FOR TODAY

We are to live as representatives of God's goodness and compassion.

WISDOM FROM SCRIPTURE

Are we beginning to commend ourselves again? Or do we need, like some people, letters of recommendation to you or from you?

You yourselves are our letter, written on our hearts, known and read by everybody.

You show that you are a letter from Christ, the result of our ministry, written not with ink but with the Spirit of the living God, not on tablets of stone but on tablets of human hearts.

Such confidence as this is ours through Christ before God.

Not that we are competent to claim anything for ourselves, but our competence comes from God.

He has made us competent as ministers of a new covenant—not of the letter but of the Spirit; for the letter kills, but the Spirit gives life.

Now if the ministry that brought death, which was engraved in letters on stone, came with glory, so that the Israelites could not look steadily at the face of Moses because of its glory, fading though it was, will not the ministry of the Spirit be even more glorious?

If the ministry that condemns men is glorious, how much more glorious is the ministry that brings righteousness!

For what was glorious has no glory now in comparison with the surpassing glory.

And if what was fading away came with glory, how much greater is the glory of that which lasts!

Therefore, since we have such a hope, we are very bold.

2 CORINTHIANS 3:1-12, NIV

INSIGHTS FROM SMITH WIGGLESWORTH

In this passage we have one of those high-water marks of very deep things of God. I believe the Lord will reveal to us these truths as our hearts are open and responsive to the Spirit's teaching. The Lord of Hosts camps round about us with "songs of deliverance" that we may see face to face the glory of His grace in a new way. For God has not brought us into cunningly devised fables, but is rolling away the mists and clouds and every difficulty that we may understand His mind and will.

If we are going to receive the best from God, there must be a spiritual desire, an open ear, an understanding heart. The veil must be lifted. We must see that God has nothing for us on the old lines. The new plan, the new revelation, the new victories are before us. New ground must be gained; supernatural things must be attained. All carnal things, evil powers, and spiritual wickedness must be dethroned.

I will dwell for a few moments on these beautiful words taken from the Scriptures which I have read to you: "Ye are our epistle [letter] written in our hearts, known and read of all men: Forasmuch as you are manifestly declared to be the epistle of Christ ministered by us, written not with ink, but with the Spirit of the living God; not in tables of stone, but in fleshly tables of the heart" (2 Cor 3:2-3).

What an ideal position in that God's glory is being revealed, the Word of God is becoming an expressed purpose in life, until the Word begins to live in these Christians and they become epistles of Christ. How true this position was in the life of Paul when he said, "I am crucified with Christ: nevertheless I live; yet not I, but Christ liveth in me: and the life which I now live in the flesh I live by faith in the Son of God, who loved me, and gave himself for me" (Gal 2:20).

How can Christ live in you? There is no way for Christ to live in you except by the manifested Word in you and through you, declaring every day that you are a living epistle of the Word of God, the living Christ, the divine likeness of God. The Word is the only factor that works within you and brings forth these glories of identification between you and Christ. Everything that comes to us must be quickened by the Spirit. Remember that "the letter killeth, but the spirit giveth life" (2 Cor 3:6). We must have life in everything.

It is true that the commandments were written on tables of stone. Moses had a heart full of joy because God had shown him a plan where Israel could partake of great things through these commandments. But now God says, "Not in tables of stone," which made the face of Moses shine with great joy. Deeper than that, more wonderful than that, His commandments are now written in our hearts. We know His deep love and compassion, eternity rolling in and bringing God in.

Oh, beloved, let God the Holy Spirit have His way today in unfolding to you the grandeur of His glory. "Not that we are sufficient of ourselves to think any thing as of ourselves; but our sufficiency is of God" (2 Cor 3:5). Ah, it is lovely!

Beloved, there is a climax of divine exaltation that is so different from human exaltation. We want to get to a place where we are beyond trusting in ourselves. There is so much failure in self-assurance. We must never rest in anything human. Our trust is in God. When we have no confidence to trust in ourselves, but when our whole trust rests upon the authority of the mighty God, He has promised to be with us at all times and to make our paths straight and to remove the mountains.

We have no confidence in the flesh. Our confidence can be only in the One who never fails, who knows the end from the beginning, who is able to come in at the midnight hour as easily as at noonday. He makes the night and day alike to the person who rests completely in the will of God, knowing that all things work together for good to those who love Him.

We cannot define, separate, or deeply investigate and unfold this holy plan of God unless we have the life of God—the thought of God, the Spirit of God, and the revelation of God. The Word of truth is pure, spiritual, and divine. We must know that the baptism of the Spirit immerses into an intensity of zeal, into a likeness to Jesus that makes us pure, molten metal, so hot for God that it travels like oil from vessel to vessel.

There is not a natural thought that can be of any use here. There is not a thing that is carnal, earthly, or natural that can live if one has this experience. The human has to die eternally because there is no other plan for a Spirit-baptized soul. God help us to see that it is possible to be filled with the letter of the Word without being filled with the Spirit. We may be filled with knowledge without having divine knowledge. No one is able to walk this way without being in the Spirit.

We must live in the Spirit, realizing all the time that we are growing in that same ideal of our Master, in season and out of season, always beholding the face of Jesus.

The Anointing of His Spirit

Questions to Consider

1. Do you feel you're a living epistle for Christ? Why or why not?

2. As a living epistle, what would you like to say to those around you?

A Prayerful Response

Lord, make me a living epistle of Your goodness and compassion. Amen.

A HOLY PASSION

THOUGHT FOR TODAY

God replaces a desire for sin with a passion for Himself.

WISDOM FROM SCRIPTURE

How great is the love the Father has lavished on us, that we should be called children of God! And that is what we are! The reason the world does not know us is that it did not know him.

Dear friends, now we are children of God, and what we will be has not yet been made known. But we know that when he appears, we shall be like him, for we shall see him as he is.

Everyone who has this hope in him purifies himself, just as he is pure.

Everyone who sins breaks the law; in fact, sin is lawlessness.

But you know that he appeared so that he might take away our sins. And in him is no sin.

No one who lives in him keeps on sinning. No one who continues to sin has either seen him or known him.

Dear children, do not let anyone lead you astray. He who does what is right is righteous, just as he is righteous.

He who does what is sinful is of the devil, because the devil has been sinning from the beginning. The reason the Son of God appeared was to destroy the devil's work.

No one who is born of God will continue to sin, because God's seed remains in him; he cannot go on sinning, because he has been born of God.

This is how we know who the children of God are and

who the children of the devil are: Anyone who does not do what is right is not a child of God; nor is anyone who does not love his brother.

1 JOHN 3:1-10, NIV

INSIGHTS FROM SMITH WIGGLESWORTH

All the wonderful things Jesus did were done that people might be changed and made like Himself. He went about His Father's business and was eaten up with the zeal of His house. Oh, to be like Him in thought, act, and plan!

I am beginning to understand 1 John 3:2: "Beloved, now are we the sons of God, and it doth not yet appear what we shall be: but we know that, when he shall appear, we shall be like him; for we shall see him as he is." As I feed on the Word of God, my whole body will be changed by the power of the Son of God. "But if the Spirit of him that raised up Jesus from the dead dwell in you, he that raised up Christ from the dead shall also quicken your mortal bodies by his Spirit that dwelleth in you" (Rom 8:11).

The Lord dwells in a humble and contrite heart and makes His way into the dry places, so if we open up to Him, He will flood us with His life. But remember that a little bit of sin will spoil a whole new life. We can never cleanse sin, be strong while in sin, or have a vision while in sin. Revelation stops when sin comes in.

The human spirit must come to an end, but the spirit of Christ must be alive and active. We must die to the human spirit, and then God will quicken our mortal body and make it alive.

When God moves a person, his body becomes akin with celestial glory, and he says things as he is led by the Holy Spirit who fills him. When we are filled with the Holy Spirit we go forth to see things accomplished that we could never see otherwise.

Paul had a vision. There is always a vision in the baptism of the Spirit. But visions are no good unless I make them real, unless I claim them, unless I make them my own. If our whole desire is to carry out what the Spirit has revealed to us by vision, it will surely come to pass.

Many people lack power because they do not allow the fire to burn continuously. There must be a continuous burning on the altar. The Holy Spirit's power in a person is meant to be an increasing force, an enlargement. God's work is never of a diminishing type; He is always going on. We must not stop in the plains; there are far greater things for us on the hilltops than in the plains.

God can make us overcomers, destroying the power and passion of sin. He can dwell in us by His mighty power and transform our lives until we love righteousness and hate iniquity.

We receive sonship because of His obedience and because of His loyalty. Do not forget, either, what the Scripture says: "Though he were a Son, yet learned he obedience by the things which he suffered" (Heb 5:8). If you turn to the Scripture, you will see that His kindred came and said, "He is possessed by Beelzebub the devil, and is doing his works" (Lk 11:15, NRSV).

See how He suffered. They reviled Him, and they tried to kill Him by throwing Him over the cliff, but He passed through the midst of the crowd and as soon as He passed through He saw a blind man and healed him.

This power of the new creation, this birth unto righteousness by faith in the atonement, can so transform and change you that you can be in Christ Jesus and know that the Spirit's power is dominating, controlling, and filling you—making you understand that though you are still in the body you are governed by the Spirit.

What a holy life! What a zeal! What a passion!

Only Believe!

QUESTIONS TO CONSIDER
1. In what ways can you express your passion for God?
2. How can you know a zeal for God is real?

A PRAYERFUL RESPONSE
Lord, give me a passion for You and Your will. Amen.

THE REWARDS OF OBEDIENCE

THOUGHT FOR TODAY

Obedience to God yields rewards beyond our imagination.

WISDOM FROM SCRIPTURE

After Jesus and his disciples arrived in Capernaum, the collectors of the two-drachma tax came to Peter and asked, "Doesn't your teacher pay the temple tax?"

"Yes, he does," he replied.

When Peter came into the house, Jesus was the first to speak. "What do you think, Simon?" he asked. "From whom do the kings of the earth collect duty and taxes—from their own sons or from others?"

"From others," Peter answered.

"Then the sons are exempt," Jesus said to him. "But so that we may not offend them, go to the lake and throw out your line. Take the first fish you catch; open its mouth and you will find a four-drachma coin. Take it and give it to them for my tax and yours."

At that time the disciples came to Jesus and asked, "Who is the greatest in the kingdom of heaven?"

He called a little child and had him stand among them.

And he said: "I tell you the truth, unless you change and become like little children, you will never enter the kingdom of heaven.

"Therefore, whoever humbles himself like this child is the greatest in the kingdom of heaven.

"And whoever welcomes a little child like this in my name welcomes me."

MATTHEW 17:24-18:5, NIV

Many things happened in the lives of the apostles to show them that the Lord Jesus had power over all flesh. In regard to paying tribute, Jesus said to Peter, "We are free, we can enter the city without paying tribute; nevertheless, we will pay" (Mt 17:26-27).

I like that thought, that Jesus told Peter to do a very hard thing. He said, "Go thou to the sea, and cast an hook, and take up the fish that first cometh up; and when thou hast opened his mouth, thou shalt find a piece of money: that take and give unto them for me and thee" (verse 27).

No doubt many things were in Peter's mind that day, but thank God there was one fish, and Peter obeyed. Sometimes to obey in blindness brings the victory. Sometimes when perplexities arise in our mind, obedience means God works out the problem.

Peter cast the hook into the sea, and it would have been amazing to have seen the disturbance the other fish made to move out of the way, all except the right one. God wanted one fish among the millions.

God may place His hand upon you in the midst of millions of people. But if He speaks to you, what He says will be appointed.

Let us think about the fullness of the Spirit, and of what God is able to do through us when we are yielded to Him. We gather in His name to kindle one another with a holier zeal than has ever possessed us before. I believe there is a greater need for this now than ever before. There are more broken spirits in our land than there have been for a long time, and no one can meet the need today but a person filled with God.

Just as the sun by its mighty power brings certain resources to nature, so I believe that the power of God in the human soul is capable, by living faith, of bringing about what otherwise could never be accomplished. May God prepare us to minister to others through His Spirit.

There are so many wonderful things about a life filled with the Holy Spirit. There are so many opportunities and such great forces that can come from no other place. When Jesus would not make bread for Himself, He made bread for thousands. And when I will not do anything for myself, God will do something for me, and then I will gladly do anything for Him that He wants.

This is the purpose of the baptism of the Holy Spirit. It creates yielded and obedient men and women.

As believers we have trusted in Christ toward God: "Not that we are sufficient of ourselves, to think anything as of ourselves, but our sufficiency is of God" (2 Cor 3:4-5). Those verses are too deep to pass over. Here is a climax of revelation that is so different from human exaltation. We want to get to a place where we are beyond trusting in ourselves.

Beloved, there is so much failure in self-assurance. We must never rest upon anything that is human. Our trust is in God, and God brings us into victory. When we have no confidence in ourselves, then our whole trust rests upon the authority of the mighty God. He has promised to be with us at all times, and to make the path straight, and to make a way through the mountains.

We can sing the words from this old hymn (Edward Mote):

> My hope is built on nothing less
> than Jesus' blood and righteousness;
> I dare not trust the sweetest frame
> but wholly lean on Jesus' name.

Our confidence can only be stayed on the One who never fails, the One who knows the end from the beginning. The day and night are alike to the man who rests completely in the will of God knowing that "all things work together for good to them that love God" (Rom 8:28). *Only Believe*

QUESTIONS TO CONSIDER

1. For you, what is difficult about blindly obeying God?
2. What are the rewards you've received for this type of obedience?

A PRAYERFUL RESPONSE

Lord, I will trust and obey You, even when I don't know the outcome. Amen.

DAY 22

DEFEATING THE THIEF

THOUGHT FOR TODAY

We can overcome the thief who wants to destroy our power in the Spirit.

WISDOM FROM SCRIPTURE

"I tell you the truth, the man who does not enter the sheep pen by the gate, but climbs in by some other way, is a thief and a robber.

"The man who enters by the gate is the shepherd of his sheep.

"The watchman opens the gate for him, and the sheep listen to his voice. He calls his own sheep by name and leads them out.

"When he has brought out all his own, he goes on ahead of them, and his sheep follow him because they know his voice.

"But they will never follow a stranger; in fact, they will run away from him because they do not recognize a stranger's voice."

Jesus used this figure of speech, but they did not understand what he was telling them.

Therefore Jesus said again, "I tell you the truth, I am the gate for the sheep.

"All who ever came before me were thieves and robbers, but the sheep did not listen to them.

"I am the gate; whoever enters through me will be saved. He will come in and go out, and find pasture.

"The thief comes only to steal and kill and destroy; I have come that they may have life, and have it to the full.

"I am the good shepherd. The good shepherd lays down his life for the sheep."

JOHN 10:1-11, NIV

INSIGHTS FROM SMITH WIGGLESWORTH

After Jesus had been transfigured on the mountain, He returned to the valley. There He found a man whose son was in a desperate condition. A devil had taken the boy and thrown him down and bruised him (see Mt 17:14-21).

The tenth chapter of John says, "The thief cometh not, but for to steal, and to kill, and to destroy: I am come that they might have life, and that they might have it more abundantly" (Jn 10:10). The thief cometh, but don't you see that the thief, the devil, comes to destroy you? Jesus came to give you life and life more abundant.

When He came down among the crowd, the father cried out, "Help me, Lord, help me. Here is my son; the devil taketh him and teareth him till he foams at the mouth, and there he lies prostrate. I brought him to Thy disciples, but they could not help me" (verses 15-16).

Oh, friend, may God strengthen your hands and take away your unbelief. Jesus said, "O faithless generation, how long shall I be with you? How long shall I suffer you? Bring him unto me" (Mk 9:19). And they brought him unto Him. And Jesus cast out the evil spirit.

Our Lord has come. Bless His name; has He come to you? He wants to come to you. He wants to share in your whole life. He wants to transform your life through His power.

Jesus was manifested to destroy the works of the devil. God so manifested His fullness in Jesus that He walked this earth glorified and filled with God. He was with God and was called the Word. He and God became one, so much so that in their operation people said it was God. Their cooperation of oneness was so manifest that there was nothing done without the other. They cooperated in the working of power.

Before the foundation of the world and before the Fall, this plan of redemption was all completed and set in order. This redemption had to be mighty to redeem us all so perfectly. There was no lack in the whole plan.

Let us see how it came about. First Jesus became flesh; then He was filled with the Holy Spirit; then He became the voice and the operation of the Word by the power of God, through the Holy Spirit. He became the authority.

Are you confident in His redemption today? If you will only believe it, you are secure. For there is a greater power in you than in all the world.

John the Baptist is commonly called the forerunner of Jesus. Within his own short history, he had the power of God revealed to him as probably no other man in the old dispensation. He had a wonderful revelation, a mighty anointing. He moved Israel as the power of God rested upon him. God gave him a vision of Jesus, and he went forth with power and turned the hearts of Israel to God.

Have you noticed how satanic power can work in the mind? Look how Satan came to John when he was in prison. I find that Satan can come to any of us. Unless we are filled with the Spirit or divinely insulated with the power of God, we may fall by the power of Satan. But we have a greater power than Satan's, in imagination, in thought, in everything.

Satan came to John the Baptist in prison, and said: "Don't you think you have made a mistake? Here you are in prison. You hear nothing about Jesus. Isn't there something wrong with the whole business? After all, you may be greatly deceived about being a forerunner of the Christ."

I find men who might be giants of faith or leaders of society, who might rise to subdue kingdoms or be noble among princes, but they go down because they allow the suggestions of Satan to dethrone their better knowledge of the power of God.

God help us today! And He will. *Only Believe!*

QUESTIONS TO CONSIDER

1. How does the devil try to steal and destroy your spiritual life?
2. In what ways can you fight off his attacks?

A PRAYERFUL RESPONSE

Lord, teach me to recognize the spiritual thief and thwart his tactics. Amen.

ALONE WITH GOD

THOUGHT FOR TODAY

To grow spiritually, it is essential to spend time alone with God.

WISDOM FROM SCRIPTURE

That night Jacob got up and took his two wives, his two maidservants and his eleven sons and crossed the ford of the Jabbok.

After he had sent them across the stream, he sent over all his possessions.

So Jacob was left alone, and a man wrestled with him till daybreak.

When the man saw that he could not overpower him, he touched the socket of Jacob's hip so that his hip was wrenched as he wrestled with the man.

Then the man said, "Let me go, for it is daybreak."

But Jacob replied, "I will not let you go unless you bless me."

The man asked him, "What is your name?"

"Jacob," he answered.

Then the man said, "Your name will no longer be Jacob, but Israel, because you have struggled with God and with men and have overcome."

Jacob said, "Please tell me your name."

But he replied, "Why do you ask my name?" Then he blessed him there.

So Jacob called the place Peniel, saying, "It is because I saw God face to face, and yet my life was spared."

The sun rose above him as he passed Peniel, and he was limping because of his hip.

Therefore to this day the Israelites do not eat the tendon attached to the socket of the hip, because the socket of Jacob's hip was touched near the tendon.

GENESIS 32:22-32, NIV

INSIGHTS FROM SMITH WIGGLESWORTH

As Jacob returned to the land of his birth, his heart was full of fear. If ever he needed the Lord it was just at this time. He had tricked his brother Esau years earlier and had never made it right; he knew his brother had vowed to kill him. Jacob wanted to be alone with God.

Oh, to be left alone! Alone with God!

In the context of Genesis 32 we read that all Jacob owned had crossed over the brook Jabbok. His wives had gone over, his children had gone over, his sheep and oxen had gone over, his camels and donkeys had gone over, all had gone over. He was alone.

The Lord saw Jacob's need and came down and met with him. It was the Lord Himself who wrestled with the supplanter (see Gen 32:24), breaking him, changing him, transforming him. Jacob was brought to a place of absolute weakness. He knew that his brother Esau had power to take away all that he owned and execute vengeance upon him. He knew there was only one kind of deliverance; no one could deliver him but God. And there alone, lean in soul and impoverished in spirit, he met with God.

Oh, we need to get alone with God, we need to be broken, we need to be changed, we need to be transformed. And when we meet with God, we need to be transformed. When we meet with God, when He interposes, all care and strife comes to an end. Get alone with God and receive the revelation of His infinite grace and of His wonderful purposes and plans for your life.

The person baptized with the Holy Spirit will always keep in touch with his Master wherever he may be. He has no room for anything that steps lower than the unction that was on his Master, or for anything that hinders him from being about his Master's business.

If you are baptized in the Holy Spirit, you have no spiritual food apart from the Word of God. You have no resources but those that are heavenly. You have been "planted" with Christ, and have risen with Him. You are seated with Him in heavenly places; your language is a heavenly language, and your source of inspiration is a heavenly touch. God is enthroned in your whole life and you see things from above, not from below.

I have seen people who used to be absolutely helpless get filled with the Holy Spirit. When the power of God took their bodies, through the Holy Spirit they became like young people instead of old withered people. This is because the Word of God is quick and powerful. Paul said, "You hath he quickened" (Eph 2:1). That quickening makes us alive, and it is powerful: "For the weapons of our warfare are not carnal, but mighty through God to the pulling down of [Satan's] strongholds" (2 Cor 10:4).

I know what Jesus meant when he said "the kingdom of heaven is within you" (Lk 17:21). He meant all those who are under the blood, who have seen the Lord by faith and know that by redemption they are children of God. The kingdom will never be complete—it could not be—until we are all there at the great supper of the Lamb where there will be millions of the redeemed, which no man can number. We shall be there when the supper is taking place.

I hope you will step into line with God and believe. It is an act of faith God wants to bring you into; a perfection of love that cannot fail. It is a fact that He has opened the kingdom of heaven to all believers and gives eternal life to them who believe.

The Lord, the Omnipotent God, knows the end from the beginning. He has arranged by the blood of the Lamb to cover the guilty and make intercession for all believers. Oh, it is a wonderful inheritance!   *Only Believe!*

QUESTIONS TO CONSIDER
1. Can you identify with Jacob's wrestling alone with God? If so, why?
2. How can you spend more time alone with God?

A PRAYERFUL RESPONSE
Lord, I will spend time alone with You, even if it is a time of spiritual wrestling. Amen.

LIFE IN THE WORD

THOUGHT FOR TODAY

We find the will of God in the Word of God.

WISDOM FROM SCRIPTURE

In the same way, the Spirit helps us in our weakness. We do not know what we ought to pray, but the Spirit himself intercedes for us with groans that words cannot express.

And he who searches our hearts knows the mind of the Spirit, because the Spirit intercedes for the saints in accordance with God's will.

And we know that in all things God works for the good of those who love him, who have been called according to his purpose.

For those God foreknew he also predestined to be conformed to the likeness of his Son, that he might be the firstborn among many brothers.

And those he predestined, he also called; those he called, he also justified; those he justified, he also glorified.

What, then, shall we say in response to this? If God is for us, who can be against us?

He who did not spare his own Son, but gave him up for us all—how will he not also, along with him, graciously give us all things?

Who will bring any charge against those whom God has chosen? It is God who justifies.

Who is he that condemns? Christ Jesus, who died—more than that, who was raised to life—is at the right hand of God and is also interceding for us.

Who shall separate us from the love of Christ? Shall

trouble or hardship or persecution or famine or nakedness or danger or sword?

As it is written: "For your sake we face death all day long; we are considered as sheep to be slaughtered."

No, in all these things we are more than conquerors through him who loved us.

ROMANS 8:26-37, NIV

INSIGHTS FROM SMITH WIGGLESWORTH

What an ideal position we are in as the children of God. Now the glory is being seen; the old life has ceased.

How truly this position was shown forth in the life of Paul when he said: "I am crucified with Christ: nevertheless I live; yet not I, but Christ liveth in me: and the life which I now live in the flesh I live by the faith of the Son of God, who loved me, and gave himself for me" (Gal 2:20).

Beloved, God would have us see that man is perfected only as the living Word abides in him. Jesus Christ is the express image of God, and the Word is the only factor that works in us to bring forth these glories of identification between us and Christ.

We may begin at Genesis, going right through the Pentateuch and the other Scriptures, and be able to rehearse them; but unless there is the living factor within us, they will be a dead letter. "The letter killeth, but the Spirit giveth life" (2 Cor 3:6).

We only know how to pray as the Spirit prays through us. The Spirit always brings to us the mind of God; He brings forth all our cries and needs; He takes the Word of God and brings our hearts and minds and souls, with all their need, into the presence of God. The Spirit prays according to the will of God, and the will of God is all in the Word of God.

A person who is baptized with the Holy Spirit has a "Jesus

mission." He knows his vocation and the plan of his life. God speaks to him so definitely that there is no mistaking it. Thank God for the knowledge that fixes him so solidly upon God's Word that he cannot be moved from it by any storm that may rage.

The revelation of Jesus to his soul by the Holy Spirit brings him to a place where he is willing, if need be, to die on what the Word says. Look at the three Hebrew children, for example, who refused to bow to the king's gods and said, "We are not careful to answer thee in this matter. If it be so, our God whom we serve is able to deliver us from the burning fiery furnace, and he will deliver us out of thine hand, O King. But if not, be it known unto thee, O King, that we will not serve thy gods, nor worship the golden image which thou hast set up" (Dn 3:16-18).

When a person is quickened by the Spirit, he never moves toward or depends upon natural resources. Even though the furnace is heated seven times hotter, it is of no consequence to the person who has heard the voice of God, and the lions' den has no fear for the person who opens his windows and talks to his Father.

People who live in the Spirit are taken out of the world in the sense that they are kept in the world without being defiled by its evil.

There is a time, though, when the preaching of the Word has no value to the hearers. Look at Hebrews 4:2: "The Word preached did not profit them, not being mixed with faith in them that heard it." May God give us faith, which quickens the preacher, the hearer, and everybody.

One day in Toronto at the close of the service I saw one of the leaders rush out as though something had happened. When I got home I found he had brought a man to me who was in a very strange way. He was a man of fine physique and looked quite all right, but his nerves were shattered; he asked me if I could do anything for a man who had not slept properly for three years.

The sleepless man said, "I have a business, a beautiful ranch and a home—it is all going. My whole nervous system is in an awful state and unless something happens, I shall lose everything." He asked for help. I said, "Go home and sleep."

He remonstrated, but I insisted that he obey my command and *go!* He went home, got into bed, fell asleep, and slept all night. In fact, he told me afterward that his wife had to wake him. He came to see me again and said, "I have slept all night; I am a new man. The whole situation is changed now."

The Word gives life and God wants it to be so alive in us that we will be moved as it is preached.

Only Believe!

QUESTIONS TO CONSIDER
1. What do you want to gain by reading God's Word?
2. How can you discern when God speaks to you through the Scriptures?

A PRAYERFUL RESPONSE
Lord, through the Scriptures reveal Your will and purpose for me. Amen.

DAY 25

THE BLESSING OF REPENTANCE

THOUGHT FOR TODAY

Personal repentance returns God's power and blessing to our lives.

WISDOM FROM SCRIPTURE

This is the message we have heard from him and declare to you: God is light; in him there is no darkness at all.

If we claim to have fellowship with him yet walk in the darkness, we lie and do not live by the truth.

But if we walk in the light, as he is in the light, we have fellowship with one another, and the blood of Jesus, his Son, purifies us from every sin.

If we claim to be without sin, we deceive ourselves and the truth is not in us.

If we confess our sins, he is faithful and just and will forgive us our sins and purify us from all unrighteousness.

If we claim we have not sinned, we make him out to be a liar and his word has no place in our lives.

My dear children, I write this to you so that you will not sin. But if anybody does sin, we have one who speaks to the Father in our defense—Jesus Christ, the Righteous One.

He is the atoning sacrifice for our sins, and not only for ours but also for the sins of the whole world.

We know that we have come to know him if we obey his commands.

The man who says, "I know him," but does not do what he commands is a liar, and the truth is not in him.

But if anyone obeys his word, God's love is truly made

complete in him. This is how we know we are in him:
Whoever claims to live in him must walk as Jesus did.

1 John 1:5-2:6, NIV

Insights from Smith Wigglesworth

Samson has his name recorded in the eleventh chapter of Hebrews as being a man of faith. He was a man who was chosen by God from his mother's womb and who had the power of God coming upon him on certain occasions.

Some people have had the power of the Lord upon them and yet they have lost out. And they know they have lost out. Friend, what about you?

God in His love and kindness put Samson in Hebrews 11, the faith chapter. There came a time when, because of Samson's sin, the Philistines were able to cut his hair, tie him with cords, and put out his eyes. As a result, he lost his strength.

He tried to break the cords but the Philistines had him secure. After his hair grew again, the Philistines wanted him to make sport for them, but he prayed and God answered.

Oh, that we might turn to God and pray this prayer: "O Lord God, remember me, I pray thee, and strengthen me, I pray thee, only this once, O God" (Jgs 16:28). If you will turn to God with true repentance, He is plenteous in mercy and He will forgive you. Repentance means getting back to God. When Samson took hold of the pillars upon which the house stood, he pulled the walls down.

God can give you strength and He will work through you. No matter what kind of a backslider you have been, there is power in the blood. "The blood of Jesus Christ his Son cleanseth us from all sin" (1 Jn 1:7).

You must live in the fire; you must hate sin; you must love righteousness; you must live with God, for He says you must be blameless and harmless amidst the crooked positions of the world. Beloved, God is able to confirm all you have heard and read about going through testings, which are the greatest blessings you can have.

God wants to make you like Jesus. Think about the loftiness of the character of Jesus, who was a firstfruit to make us pure and holy. I see Jesus going about clothed with power. And I see you, a child of God, clothed with power. Jesus was a firstfruit, the pattern of God.

In Jesus, God has not given you a pattern which is impossible to copy. Beloved, Jesus hated sin. If you have hatred for sin, you have something worth millions. Oh, the blood of Jesus Christ, God's Son, cleanses us from all sin.

I believe that the hope of the Church for the future is in its being purified—made like unto Jesus, pure in heart, pure in thought. Then, when a believer lays hands upon the sick, Satan has no power; when he commands him to leave, Satan has to go.

Jacob is a good example of a person who had to get rid of a lot of things when he met God at Peniel (see Gn 32:24-30). It had been all Jacob! Jacob!

Hour after hour passed. Oh, that we might spend all night alone with God! We are occupied too much with the things of time and sense. We need the presence of God. We need to give God time if we are to receive new revelations from Him. We need to get past all the thoughts of earthly matters that crowd in so rapidly. We need to give God time to deal with us. It is only after He has dealt with us, as He dealt with Jacob, that we can have power through Him and prevail.

Jacob was not dry-eyed that night. Hosea tells us, "He wept and made supplication" (Hos 12:4). He knew he had been a disappointment to the Lord; he had been a groveler.

But in the revelation he received as he wrestled that night, there was the possibility of being transformed from a supplanter to a prince of God.

The testing hour came when at break of day the angel, who was none other than the Lord of Hosts, said to him, "Let me go, for the day breaketh" (Gn 32:26). Jacob knew that if God left without blessing him, he could not meet Esau. Likewise, you cannot meet the terrible things that await you in the world unless you receive the blessing of God.

Seek Him today! *Only Believe!*

QUESTIONS TO CONSIDER

1. Are you missing spiritual power in your life? If so, how does this affect your daily life?
2. To return to a power-filled life, what might you need to repent of today?

A PRAYERFUL RESPONSE

Lord, I repent of my sin and waywardness. Bless me and refill me with Your power. Amen.

MAKING A PEST OF YOURSELF

THOUGHT FOR TODAY

If we desire something according to God's will, we're to keep asking for it.

WISDOM FROM SCRIPTURE

"Ask and it will be given to you; seek and you will find; knock and the door will be opened to you.

"For everyone who asks receives; he who seeks finds; and to him who knocks, the door will be opened.

"Which of you, if his son asks for bread, will give him a stone? Or if he asks for a fish, will give him a snake?

"If you, then, though you are evil, know how to give good gifts to your children, how much more will your Father in heaven give good gifts to those who ask him!

"So in everything, do to others what you would have them do to you, for this sums up the Law and the Prophets.

"Enter through the narrow gate. For wide is the gate and broad is the road that leads to destruction, and many enter through it. But small is the gate and narrow the road that leads to life, and only a few find it.

"Watch out for false prophets. They come to you in sheep's clothing, but inwardly they are ferocious wolves.

"By their fruit you will recognize them. Do people pick grapes from thornbushes, or figs from thistles?

"Likewise every good tree bears good fruit, but a bad tree bears bad fruit.

"A good tree cannot bear bad fruit, and a bad tree cannot bear good fruit. Every tree that does not bear good fruit is cut down and thrown into the fire.

"Thus, by their fruit you will recognize them."

MATTHEW 7:7-20, NIV

INSIGHTS FROM SMITH WIGGLESWORTH

What would happen to us and to the needy world if we should get to the place where we really believed God? May God give us the desire to get to this place. Faith is a tremendous power, an inward mover. I am convinced that we have not yet seen all that God has for us, but if we shall only move on faith, we shall see the greater works.

When I was a little boy I remember asking my father for a pennyworth of something or other. He did not give it to me, so I sat down by his side and every now and again I would just quietly say, "Father!" He would appear to take no notice of me, but now and again I would touch him ever so gently and say, "Father!"

My mother said to him, "Why don't you answer the child?"

My father replied, "I have done so, but he won't accept my answer."

Still I sat there, and occasionally I would touch him and say, ever so quietly, "Father!" If he went out into the garden I followed him, and occasionally I would touch his sleeve and say, "Father! Father!"

Do you think I ever went away without the accomplishment of my desire? No, not once. We need the same importunity as we go to God. We have the blessed assurance that if we ask anything according to His will He hears us. And if we know that God hears us, whatsoever we ask, we know that we have the petitions we desire of Him.

Do you go to God for purity of heart? It is His will that

you should receive it, and if you ask in faith you can know you have the petition you desire of Him. Do you desire that Christ should dwell in your heart by faith? That is in accordance with His will. Ask and you shall receive. Do you desire that the might of God's Spirit shall accompany your ministry? That is according to the will of God.

Continue in the presence of your heavenly Father, quietly reminding Him that this is what you desire, and He will not fail to give you an exceeding abundance, above all you ask or think. He will fill you with rivers—the blessed rivers of the Spirit—and flowing from the midst of you, they will be blessings to all around.

Do you remember how they asked the Lord, "What shall we do, that we might work the works of God?" Jesus answered, "This is the work of God, that ye believe on him whom he hath sent" (Jn 6:28-29). He further said, "The works that I do shall [you] do also; and greater works than these shall [you] do; because I go unto my Father" (Jn 14:12). There is nothing impossible to faith.

When I was in Sweden years ago I ministered to a blind girl who was twelve years old. She had perfect sight from that day. The Lord Himself challenges us to believe Him when He says, "Have faith in God." He says, "Verily I say unto you, that whosoever shall say to this mountain, Be thou removed, and be thou cast into the sea, and shall not doubt in his heart, but shall believe that those things which he saith shall come to pass; he shall have whatsoever he saith" (Mk 11:23).

Did you get that? "He shall have whatsoever he says." When you speak in faith, your desire is an accomplished thing. Our Lord added, "Therefore I say unto you, What things soever you desire, when ye pray, believe that ye receive them, and ye shall have them" (verse 24).

Have you received this faith? If so, deal bountifully with the oppressed. God has called us to loose the bonds of wickedness, undo the heavy burden, let the oppressed go free, and break the yokes that the devil has put upon them. Pray in faith.

Remember: those who ask receive. Ask and it shall be given to you. Live for God. Keep yourself clean and holy. Live under the unction of the Holy Spirit. Let the mind of Christ be yours so that you live in God's desires and plans.

Glorify God in the establishment of His blessing upon the people, and in seeing His glory manifested in our midst.

The Anointing of His Spirit

QUESTIONS TO CONSIDER
1. What burning request do you have for God?
2. Will you keep asking for this request according to God's will? Why or why not?

A PRAYERFUL RESPONSE
Lord, by faith I ask that You fulfill my requests according to Your will. Amen.

DAY 27

LOVE ONE ANOTHER

THOUGHT FOR TODAY
If God dwells in us, we will love others as He does.

WISDOM FROM SCRIPTURE
Dear friends, let us love one another, for love comes from God. Everyone who loves has been born of God and knows God.

Whoever does not love does not know God, because God is love.

This is how God showed his love among us: He sent his one and only Son into the world that we might live through him.

This is love: not that we loved God, but that he loved us and sent his Son as an atoning sacrifice for our sins.

Dear friends, since God so loved us, we also ought to love one another.

No one has ever seen God; but if we love one another, God lives in us and his love is made complete in us.

We know that we live in him and he in us, because he has given us of his Spirit.

And we have seen and testify that the Father has sent his Son to be the Savior of the world.

If anyone acknowledges that Jesus is the Son of God, God lives in him and he in God. And so we know and rely on the love God has for us.

God is love. Whoever lives in love lives in God, and God in him. In this way, love is made complete among us so that we will have confidence on the day of judgment, because in this world we are like him.

There is no fear in love. But perfect love drives out fear, because fear has to do with punishment. The one who fears is not made perfect in love.

We love because he first loved us.

If anyone says, "I love God," yet hates his brother, he is a liar. For anyone who does not love his brother, whom he has seen, cannot love God, whom he has not seen.

And he has given us this command: Whoever loves God must also love his brother.

1 JOHN 4:7-21, NIV

INSIGHTS FROM SMITH WIGGLESWORTH

It is always a very blessed time for believers to gather for communion in remembrance of the Lord. Jesus said, "This do in remembrance of Me" (1 Cor 11:24).

When we gather to commemorate our Lord's wonderful death, victory, and triumph, and look forward to the glorious hope, we need to get rid of our religion. It has always been religion that has slain and destroyed what was good.

Sad as it is to say, when Satan entered into Judas, the only people the devil could speak to through Judas were the priests. They conspired to get him to betray Jesus, and the devil took money from these priests to put Jesus to death.

Now it is a very serious thing, for we must clearly understand whether we are of the right spirit or not, for no man can be of the spirit of Christ and persecute another. No person can have the true spirit of Jesus and slay his brother, and no one can follow the Lord Jesus and have enmity in his heart. You cannot have Jesus and have bitterness and hatred.

Do you want a new commandment, one that will change your life and that of others? You'll find it in John 13:34-35: "A new commandment I give unto you, that ye love one another; as I have loved you, that ye also love one another. By this shall all men know that ye are my disciples, if ye have love one to another."

I'll never forget when we had our first baby. While he slept in the cradle, my wife and I both went to him and my wife would say, "I cannot bear to have him sleep any longer. I want him." And I remember waking the baby because she wanted him. "If ye then, being evil, know how to give good gifts unto your children; how much more shall your heavenly Father give the Holy Spirit to them that ask him?" (Lk 11:13).

Ah, he is such a lovely Father.

One time I thought I had the Holy Spirit. Now I know the Holy Spirit has got me. There is a difference between our hanging on to God and God lifting us up. There is a difference between my having a desire and God's desire filling my soul. There is a difference between natural compassion and the compassion of Jesus that never fails. Human faith fails but the faith of Jesus never fails.

Oh, beloved, I see through these glorious truths a new dawning: churches loving one another, all of one accord. Until that time comes there will be deficiencies. "By this shall all men know that ye are my disciples, if ye have love one to another" (Jn 13:35).

Love is the secret and center of the divine position. Where are your boundaries today? There are heights and depths and lengths and breadths to the love of God. The Word of God contains the principles of life. I live not, but another mightier than I lives in me. The desires have gone into the desire of God.

Oh, how God loves His children!

"And now abideth faith, hope, charity [love], these three; but the greatest of these is charity. Follow after charity, and desire spiritual gifts, but rather that ye may prophesy. For he that speaketh in an unknown tongue speaketh not unto men, but unto God; for no man understandeth him; howbeit in the spirit he speaketh mysteries. But he that prophesieth speaketh unto men to edification, and exhortation, and comfort" (1 Cor 13:13-14:3).

When love is in perfect progress, other things will work in harmony, for prophetic utterances are of no value unless perfectly covered by divine love.

Jesus was so full of love to His Father and love to us that His love never failed to accomplish its purpose. It works in us and through us by the power of the Father's love in Him. This is what must come into our lives.

Only Believe!

QUESTIONS TO CONSIDER
1. Is there anyone you find difficult to love? If so, why?
2. How can you bring God's love into this relationship?

A PRAYERFUL RESPONSE
Lord, help me love others as You love me. Amen.

DAY 28

The Truth about Sanctification

Thought for Today

If we let Him, God will purify us for a deeper relationship with Him.

Wisdom from Scripture

Peter, an apostle of Jesus Christ, to God's elect, strangers in the world, scattered throughout Pontus, Galatia, Cappadocia, Asia and Bithynia, who have been chosen according to the foreknowledge of God the Father, by the sanctifying work of the Spirit, for obedience to Jesus Christ and sprinkling by his blood: Grace and peace be yours in abundance.

Praise be to the God and Father of our Lord Jesus Christ! In his great mercy he has given us new birth into a living hope through the resurrection of Jesus Christ from the dead, and into an inheritance that can never perish, spoil or fade—kept in heaven for you, who through faith are shielded by God's power until the coming of the salvation that is ready to be revealed in the last time.

In this you greatly rejoice, though now for a little while you may have had to suffer grief in all kinds of trials.

These have come so that your faith—of greater worth than gold, which perishes even though refined by fire—may be proved genuine and may result in praise, glory and honor when Jesus Christ is revealed.

Though you have not seen him, you love him; and even though you do not see him now, you believe in him and are filled with an inexpressible and glorious joy, for you are receiving the goal of your faith, the salvation of your souls.

1 Peter 1:1-9, NIV

I want you to notice that in all times, in all histories of the world, whenever there has been a divine rising or revelation (God coming forth with a new dispensational order of the Spirit), there have been persecutions. What for? Because of things very much against the revelations of God and the Spirit of God.

Humanity, flesh, natural things are against divine things. Evil powers work upon this position of the human life, especially when the will is unyielded to God. Then the powers of darkness rise up against the powers of divine order; but they never defeat them.

Divine order is often in minority, yet always in majority. Did I say that right? Yes, and I meant it also. You have no need to fear; truth stands eternal. Wickedness may increase and abound, but when the Lord raises His flag over the saint, it is victory; though it is in minority, it always triumphs.

I want you to notice the first verse in this passage (see 1 Pt 1:1-9) because it says *scattered*, meaning they did not get much of the liberty of meeting together. They were driven from place to place. Even in the days of John Knox, the people who served God had to be in close quarters because they were persecuted, hauled before judges, and destroyed in all sorts of ways. They were in the minority but swept through in victory. May God bring us into perfect order so we understand we may be in minority, yet in majority.

The Holy Spirit wants us to understand our privileges according to the foreknowledge of God through the sanctification of the Spirit. Now these words "sanctification of the Spirit" are not on the lines of sin cleansing; it is a higher order than redemption work. The blood of Jesus is rich unto all, powerful and cleansing. It takes away other powers and transforms us by the power of God. When sin is gone, when we are clean and know we have the Word of God in us and the power of the Spirit bringing us to a place where we triumph, then comes revelation by the power of the Spirit lifting us to higher ground, into the fullness of God, unveiling Christ. It is called sanctification of the Spirit.

I don't want you to stumble at the word *elect;* it is a blessed word. You might say you are all elect; everyone in this place could say you are elected. God has designed that all people should be saved—this is election. Whether you accept and come into your election, whether you prove yourself worthy of your election, whether you have done this, I don't know; but this is your election, your sanctification, to be seated at the right hand of God.

The word *election* is a very precious word. To be fore-ordained, predestined—these are words that God has designed to bring us into triumph and victory in Christ. Some people play around and make it a goal. They say, "Oh, well, you see, we are elected. We are all right." They say they are elected to be saved, and I believe they are very diplomatic because they believe others can be elected to be damned. It is not true! Everybody is elected to be saved, but whether they come into it or not is another thing. Many don't come into salvation because the god of this world has blinded their eyes lest the light of the glorious gospel should shine into them.

What does this mean? It means this: Satan has mastery over their minds, and they listen to corruptible things.

I want you to see this election I am speaking about, to catch a glimpse of heaven where you grasp everything spiritual, where everything divine makes you hungry, and everything seasonable in spiritual fidelity makes you long after it. If I came here in a year's time I should see this kind of election going forward, always full, never having a bad report, where you see Christ every day and grow in the knowledge of God.

It is through sanctification of the Spirit unto obedience and sprinkling of the blood of Jesus Christ. There is no sanctification if it is not sanctification unto obedience. There would be no trouble with any of us if we would come definitely to a place where we understood the words that Jesus said: "For their sakes I sanctify myself, that they might be sanctified through the truth" (Jn 17:19).

Through sanctification of the Spirit, you will get to a place where you are not disturbed. There is a peace in sanctification because it leads to revelation and takes you into heavenly places where God speaks and makes Himself known to you. When you are face to face with God, you get a peace which passes all understanding, lifting you from state to state of inexpressible wonderment.

It is really wonderful!

Smith Wigglesworth: A Man Who Walked with God

QUESTIONS TO CONSIDER

1. Before today, what has been your understanding of sanctification?
2. Have you experienced the sanctification described in this reading?

A PRAYERFUL RESPONSE

Lord, sanctify me with Your Spirit. Bring me into a deeper relationship with You. Amen.

PART FOUR

FOLLOWING GOD'S CALL

A woman came to me one day and said,

"My husband is such a trial to me. The first salary he gets he spends it
on drink and then he cannot do his work and comes home.

I love him very much. What can be done?"

I said, "If I were you I would [follow Apostle Paul's example].

Take a handkerchief and place it under his head when he goes to sleep at
night, and say nothing to him, but have a living faith."

We anointed a handkerchief in the name of Jesus, and she put it under
his head.

The next morning on his way to work her husband stopped for a glass of
beer.

He lifted it to his lips but he thought there was something wrong with it;
so he put it down and went out.

He went to another saloon, and another, and did the same thing.

At the end of the day he came home sober.

His wife was gladly surprised to see him so, and he told her his story,
how it had affected him.

That was the turning point in this man's life.

It meant not only giving up drink, but it also meant his salvation.

THE ANOINTING OF HIS SPIRIT

SMITH WIGGLESWORTH'S INSIGHT

When we follow God's call, we become vessels for His
miracles.

DAY 29

WHAT WILL YOU HAVE ME DO?

THOUGHT FOR TODAY

Yielding to God begins with the question, "What will You have me do?"

WISDOM FROM SCRIPTURE

Now as he [Saul] was going along and approaching Damascus, suddenly a light from heaven flashed around him.

He fell to the ground and heard a voice saying to him, "Saul, Saul, why do you persecute me?"

He asked, "Who are you, Lord? The reply came, I am Jesus, whom you are persecuting. But get up and enter the city, and you will be told what you are to do."

The men who were traveling with him stood speechless because they heard the voice but saw no one.

Saul got up from the ground, and though his eyes were open, he could see nothing; so they led him by the hand and brought him into Damascus.

For three days he was without sight, and neither ate nor drank.

Now there was a disciple in Damascus named Ananias. The Lord said to him in a vision, "Ananias." He answered, "Here I am, Lord."

The Lord said to him, "Get up and go to the street called Straight, and at the house of Judas look for a man of Tarsus named Saul. At this moment he is praying, and he has seen in a vision a man named Ananias come in and lay his hands on him so that he might regain his sight."

But Ananias answered, "Lord, I have heard from many about this man, how much evil he has done to your saints in Jerusalem; and here he has authority from the chief priests to bind all who invoke your name."

But the Lord said to him, "Go, for he is an instrument whom I have chosen to bring my name before Gentiles and kings and before the people of Israel; I myself will show him how much he must suffer for the sake of my name."

ACTS 9:3-16, NRSV

INSIGHTS FROM SMITH WIGGLESWORTH

As soon as Paul saw the light from heaven outshining the brightness of the sun, he said, "Lord, what wilt thou have me to do?" (Acts 9:6). And as soon as he was willing to yield, he was in a condition where God could display His power, where God could have him.

The place of yieldedness is just where God wants us. People are saying, "I want the baptism, I want healing, I would like to know with certainty that I am a child of God." And I see nothing, absolutely nothing, in the way except unyieldedness to the plan of God. And that is what God wants from us today: obedience.

When we begin yielding to God, He is able to fulfill His plan for our lives, and we come into that wonderful place where all we have to do is eat the fruits of Canaan. But the thing God is looking for is obedience.

If God can have His way today, the ministry of somebody will begin; it always begins as soon as we yield. Paul had been bringing many people to prison, but God brought Paul to such a place of yieldedness and brokenness that he cried out, "What will You have me to do?" Paul's choice was to be a bondservant for Jesus Christ.

Are you willing that God shall have His way today? Jesus said, "I will show him how great things he must suffer for my name's sake" (Acts 9:16). But Paul saw that these things were working out a far more exceeding weight of glory. You who want a touch from God, are you willing to follow Him? Will you obey Him?

When the prodigal son had returned and the father had killed the fatted calf and made a feast for him, the elder brother was angry and complained, "Thou never gavest me a kid, that I might make merry with my friends." But the father said to him, "All that I have is thine" (Lk 15:29-31). The elder brother could kill a fatted calf any time. Beloved, all in the Father's house is ours, but it will come only through obedience. And when He can trust us, we will not come behind in anything.

Notice how God used Paul in Ephesus: "God wrought special miracles by the hands of Paul: So that from his body were brought unto the sick handkerchiefs or aprons, and the diseases departed from them, and the evil spirits went out of them" (Acts 19:11-12). Let us notice the handkerchiefs that went forth from his special miracles through them, and diseases departed from the sick, and evil spirits went out of the afflicted.

I believe that after we lay hands on these handkerchiefs and pray over them today, they should be handled very sacredly, and even as someone carries them, these handkerchiefs will bring life—if they are carried in faith to the suffering. The very effect of it, if you only believe, would change your own body as you carry it.

Who will take the place of Paul, and yield and yield, until God so possesses him that from his body virtue shall flow to the sick and suffering? It will have to be the virtue of Christ that flows. There is no magic virtue in the handkerchief; it is the living faith of the person who lays the handkerchief on the body, and the power of God through the faith.

There is another side to it. "Exorcists took upon them to call over them which had evil spirits the name of the Lord Jesus, saying, 'We adjure you by Jesus whom Paul preacheth...' And the evil spirit answered and said, "Jesus I know, and Paul I know, but who are ye?" (Acts 19:13-15). I beseech you in the name of Jesus, especially those of you who are baptized, to awaken to the fact that you have power if God is with you. But there must be a resemblance between you and Jesus. The evil spirit said, "Jesus I know, and Paul I know, but who are you?"

The difference between these men and Paul was that they had not the marks of Christ, so the manifestation of the power of Christ was not seen. Do you want power? Don't take the wrong way. Don't assume you have power because you speak in tongues. If God has given you revelations along certain lines, don't take that for power. Even if you have laid hands on the sick and they have been healed, don't take that for power.

"The Spirit of the Lord is upon me" (Lk 4:18). That alone is the power. Don't be deceived. There is a place where you know the Spirit is upon you, so you will be able to do the works which are wrought by this blessed Spirit of God in you. And the manifestation of His power shall be seen, and people will believe in the Lord.

The Anointing of His Spirit

QUESTIONS TO CONSIDER

1. In regard to yielding your life, what has God asked you to do?

2. Are you willing to keep asking, "Lord, what will You have me do?"

A PRAYERFUL RESPONSE

Lord, what will You have me do? Amen.

DELIVERANCE TO THE CAPTIVES

THOUGHT FOR TODAY

God wants to deliver us from sin's bondage so we can help deliver others.

WISDOM FROM SCRIPTURE

Then Jesus, filled with the power of the Spirit, returned to Galilee, and a report about him spread through all the surrounding country. He began to teach in their synagogues and was praised by everyone.

When he came to Nazareth, where he had been brought up, he went to the synagogue on the sabbath day, as was his custom. He stood up to read, and the scroll of the prophet Isaiah was given to him. He unrolled the scroll and found the place where it was written: "The Spirit of the Lord is upon me, because he has anointed me to bring good news to the poor. He has sent me to proclaim release to the captives and recovery of sight to the blind, to let the oppressed go free, to proclaim the year of the Lord's favor."

And he rolled up the scroll, gave it back to the attendant, and sat down. The eyes of all in the synagogue were fixed on him.

Then he began to say to them, "Today this scripture has been fulfilled in your hearing."

All spoke well of him and were amazed at the gracious words that came from his mouth. They said, "Is not this Joseph's son?"

He said to them, "Doubtless you will quote to me this proverb, 'Doctor, cure yourself!' And you will say, 'Do here also in your hometown the things that we have heard you did at Capernaum.'"

And he said, "Truly I tell you, no prophet is accepted in the prophet's hometown."

Luke 4:14-24, NRSV

Insights from Smith Wigglesworth

One day I came home from work and went into the house and my wife asked me, "Which way did you come in?" I said I came in the back door. She said, "There is a woman upstairs who has brought an old man of eighty to be prayed for. He is raving up there and a crowd is outside the front door, ringing the doorbell and wanting to know what is going on in the house."

The Lord quietly whispered to me, "This is what I baptized you for."

I carefully opened the door of the room where the man was, desiring to be obedient to what my Lord would say to me. The man was crying and shouting in distress, "I am lost! I am lost! I have committed the unpardonable sin. I am lost! I am lost!"

My wife asked, "What shall we do?"

The Spirit of the Lord moved me to cry out, "Come out, thou lying spirit!" In a moment the evil spirit went, and the man was free. Deliverance to the captives!

Then the Lord said to me again, "This is what I baptized you for."

There is a place where God, through the power of the Holy Spirit, reigns supreme in our lives. The Spirit reveals, unfolds, takes of the things of Christ, and shows them to us, preparing us to be more than a match for satanic forces.

When a person is born of God, is brought from darkness to light, a mighty miracle is wrought. Jesus saw every touch by God as a miracle, and so we may expect to see miracles wrought today. It is wonderful to have the Spirit of the Lord upon us. I would rather have the Spirit of God on me for five minutes than to receive a million dollars.

Do you see how Jesus mastered the devil in the wilderness? Jesus knew He was the Son of God and Satan came along with an "if." How many times has Satan come to you this way? He says, "After all, you may be deceived. You know you really are not a child of God." If the devil says you are not saved, it is a pretty sure sign that you are. When he tells you that you are not healed, it may be taken as good evidence that the Lord has sent His word and healed you.

The devil knows that if he can capture your thought life, he has won a mighty victory over you. His great business is injecting thoughts, but if you are pure and holy you will instantly shrink from them. God wants you to let the mind that was in Christ Jesus—that pure, holy, humble mind of Christ—be in you.

I come across people everywhere I go who are held bound by deceptive conditions, and these conditions have come about simply because they have allowed the devil to make their minds his stronghold. How are we to guard against this? The Lord has provided us with weapons that are mighty through God to the pulling down of these strongholds of the enemy, and our thoughts shall be brought into captivity to the obedience of Christ. The blood of Jesus Christ and His mighty name are an antidote to all the subtle seed of unbelief that Satan would sow in our minds.

The ministry of Christ did not end at the cross, but the Acts and the Epistles give us accounts of what He continued to do and teach through those whom He indwelt. And our blessed Lord Jesus is still alive and continues His ministry through those who are filled with His Spirit. He is still healing the brokenhearted and delivering the captives through those on whom He places His Spirit.

Oh, if we would only believe God! What would happen? The greatest things. Some have never tasted the grace of God, have never had the peace of God. Unbelief robs them of those blessings. It is possible to hear and yet not conceive the truth. It is possible to read the Word and not share in the life it brings. We need the Holy Spirit to unfold the Word and bring to us the life that is in Christ. We can never fully understand the wonders of this redemption until we are full of the Holy Spirit.

Are you oppressed? Cry out to God. It is always good for people to cry out. You may have to cry out. The Holy Spirit and the Word of God will bring to light every hidden, unclean thing that must be revealed. There is always a place of deliverance when you let God search out what is spoiling and marring your life. He is just the same Jesus, exposing the powers of evil, delivering the captives and letting the oppressed go free, purifying them and cleansing their hearts. Hell is such an awful place that even the demons hate the thought of going there. How much more should men seek to be saved from the pit?

God is compassionate and says, "Seek ye the Lord while he may be found" (Is 55:6). And He has further stated, "Whosoever shall call on the name of the Lord shall be saved" (Jl 2:32). Seek Him now, call on His name right now. There is forgiveness, healing, redemption, deliverance, and everything you need right here and now, as well as what will satisfy you throughout eternity.   *Ever Increasing Faith*

Questions to Consider

1. Are you captive to anything that needs God's deliverance? Be specific.
2. What will you need to do to be set free?

A Prayerful Response

Lord, I cry out to You, asking that You set my captive heart free. Amen.

THE POWER OF HIS NAME

THOUGHT FOR TODAY

The power of Jesus' name can change anyone or conquer anything.

WISDOM FROM SCRIPTURE

One day Peter and John were going up to the temple at the hour of prayer, at three o'clock in the afternoon.

And a man lame from birth was being carried in. People would lay him daily at the gate of the temple called the Beautiful Gate so that he could ask for alms from those entering the temple.

When he saw Peter and John about to go into the temple, he asked them for alms.

Peter looked intently at him, as did John, and said, "Look at us."

And he fixed his attention on them, expecting to receive something from them.

But Peter said, "I have no silver or gold, but what I have I give you; in the name of Jesus Christ of Nazareth, stand up and walk."

And he took him by the right hand and raised him up; and immediately his feet and ankles were made strong.

Jumping up, he stood and began to walk, and he entered the temple with them, walking and leaping and praising God.

All the people saw him walking and praising God, and they recognized him as the one who used to sit and ask for alms at the Beautiful Gate of the temple; and they were filled with wonder and amazement at what had happened to him.

While he clung to Peter and John, all the people ran together to them in the portico called Solomon's Portico, utterly astonished.

When Peter saw it, he addressed the people, "You Israelites, why do you wonder at this, or why do you stare at us, as though by our own power or piety we had made him walk?

"The God of Abraham, the God of Isaac, and the God of Jacob, the God of our ancestors has glorified his servant Jesus, whom you handed over and rejected in the presence of Pilate, though he had decided to release him.

"But you rejected the Holy and Righteous One and asked to have a murderer given to you, and you killed the Author of life, whom God raised from the dead. To this we are witnesses.

"And by faith in his name, his name itself has made this man strong, whom you see and know; and the faith that is through Jesus has given him this perfect health in the presence of all of you."

ACTS 3:1-16, NRSV

INSIGHTS FROM SMITH WIGGLESWORTH

All things are possible through the name of Jesus. God has highly exalted Him and given Him the name which is above every name, that at the name of Jesus every knee should bow (see Phil 2:10). There is power to overcome everything in the world through the name of Jesus. "There is no other name under heaven, given among men, whereby we must be saved" (Acts 4:12). I want to instill into you a sense of the power, virtue, and glory of that name.

Six people went into the house of a sick man to pray for him. He was an Episcopalian vicar, and lay in his bed utterly helpless, without even strength to help himself. He had read

a little tract about healing and had heard about people praying for the sick, so he sent for these friends who could pray
the prayer of faith. He was anointed according to James 5:14,
but because he had no immediate manifestation of healing,
he wept bitterly. The six people walked out of the room,
somewhat crestfallen to see the man in an unchanged condition.

When they were outside, one of the six said, "There is one
thing we might have done. I wish you would all go back with
me and try it." They went back and all got together in a
group. This brother said, "Let me whisper the name of
Jesus." At first when they whispered this worthy name nothing seemed to happen. But as they continued to whisper,
"Jesus! Jesus! Jesus!" the power began to fall.

As they saw that God was beginning to work, their faith
and joy increased, and they whispered the name louder and
louder. As they did so the man arose from his bed and
dressed himself. The secret was this: Those six people got
their eyes off the sick man and were taken up with the Lord
Jesus Himself, and their faith grasped the power there is in
His name. Oh, if people would only appreciate the power
there is in this name, there is no telling what would happen.

I know that through His name and through the power of
His name we have access to God. The very face of Jesus fills
the whole place with glory. All over the world there are
people magnifying that name, and oh, what a joy it is for me
to utter it.

Peter and John were helpless and illiterate; they had no
college education. But they had been with Jesus. They had
handed out the bread and fish after Jesus had multiplied
them. They had sat at the table with Him, and John had
often gazed into His face. Peter had often been rebuked, but

Jesus manifested His love to Peter through it all. He loved Peter, the wayward one.

Oh, He's a wonderful Lover! I have been wayward; I have been stubborn; I had an unmanageable bad temper at one time. But how patient He has been. I am here to tell you that there is power in Jesus and in His wondrous name to transform anyone, to heal anyone. If you will see Him as God's Lamb, as God's beloved Son who had laid upon Him the iniquity of us all, if you will see that Jesus paid the whole price for our redemption that we might be free, you can enter into your purchased inheritance of salvation, life, and power.

Poor Peter and poor John! They had no money! But they had faith; they had the power of the Holy Spirit; they had God. You can have God even though you have nothing else. Even though you have lost your character you can have God. I have seen the worst of men saved by the power of God.

The name of Jesus is so marvelous. Peter and John had no conception of all that was in that name; neither had the man, lame from his mother's womb, who was laid daily at the gate. But they had faith to say, "In the name of Jesus Christ of Nazareth, rise up and walk." And as Peter took him by the right hand and lifted him up, immediately his feet and ankle bones received strength, and he went into the temple with them, walking and leaping and praising God.

God wants you to see more of this sort of thing done. How can it be done? Through His name, through faith in His name, through faith which is by Him.

Ever Increasing Faith

Questions to Consider

1. How can you cultivate faith in the name of Jesus?
2. For what will you call on the name of Jesus today?

A Prayerful Response

Lord, I believe in the power of Your name, and will call on it for help. Amen.

DAY 32

A TOUCH OF REALITY

THOUGHT FOR TODAY

The healing touch of Jesus is a reality for us today.

WISDOM FROM SCRIPTURE

When he returned to Capernaum after some days, it was reported that he was at home.

So many gathered around that there was no longer room for them, not even in front of the door; and he was speaking the word to them.

Then some people came, bringing to him a paralyzed man, carried by four of them.

And when they could not bring him to Jesus because of the crowd, they removed the roof above him; and after having dug through it, they let down the mat on which the paralytic lay.

When Jesus saw their faith, he said to the paralytic, "Son, your sins are forgiven."

Now some of the scribes were sitting there, questioning in their hearts, "Why does this fellow speak in this way? It is blasphemy! Who can forgive sins but God alone?"

At once Jesus perceived in his spirit that they were discussing these questions among themselves; and he said to them, "Why do you raise such questions in your hearts? Which is easier, to say to the paralytic, 'Your sins are forgiven,' or to say, 'Stand up and take your mat and walk'?"

"But so that you may know that the Son of Man has authority on earth to forgive sins," he said to the paralytic, "I say to you, stand up, take your mat and go to your home."

And he stood up, and immediately took the mat and went out before all of them; so that they were all amazed and glorified God, saying, "We have never seen anything like this!"   MARK 2:1-12, NRSV

INSIGHTS FROM SMITH WIGGLESWORTH

Something ought to happen all the time so people will say, "We never saw anything like that." If there is anything with which God is dissatisfied, it is stationary conditions. So many people stop on the threshold when God in His great plan is inviting them into His treasury. Oh, this treasury of the Most High, the unsearchable riches of Christ, this divine position into which God wants to move us so we are altogether new creations!

We know that the flesh profits nothing. "The carnal mind is enmity against God; for it is not subject to the law of God, neither indeed can be" (Rom 8:7). As we cease to live in the old life and know the resurrection power of the Lord, we come into a place of rest, faith, joy, peace, blessings, and life everlasting.

May the Lord give us a new vision of Himself, a fresh touch of divine life and His presence that will shake off all that remains of the old life and bring us fully into His newness of life. May God reveal to us the greatness of His will concerning us, for there is no one who loves us like He does. Yes, there is no love like His, no compassion like His. He is filled with compassion, and never fails to take those who will fully obey Him into the Promised Land.

In God's Word there is always more to follow, always more than we know. Oh, if only we could be babies, with a child-like mind to take in all the mind of God, what wonderful things would happen! I wonder if you take the Bible just for yourself. It is grand. Never mind who takes only a part; you take it all. When you get such a thirst that nothing can satisfy you but God, you shall have a royal time.

As children of God we must have reality all the time. After we come into the sweetness of the perfume of the presence of God, we will have the hidden treasures of God and will always be feeding on that blessed truth that will make life full of glory.

Are you dry? There is no dry place in God, but all the good things come out of hard times. The harder the place you are in, the more blessedness can come out of it as you yield to His plan. Oh, if only I had known God's plan in its fullness I might never have had a tear in my life. God is so abundant, so full of love and mercy. There is no lack to those who trust in Him.

I pray that God may give us some touch of reality so we may be able to trust Him all the way. It is an ideal thing to believe that when we ask, we shall receive. But how could it be otherwise? It must be so when God says it.

I tell you, my sister, my brother, since the day Christ's blood was shed, since the day of His atonement, He has paid the price to meet all the world's need and its cry of sorrow. Truly Jesus has met the need of the broken hearts and the sorrowful spirits, and also of the withered limbs and the broken bodies. God's dear Son paid the debt for all, for He took our infirmities and bore our sicknesses. In all points He was tempted as we are, in order that He might be able to succor those who are tempted.

I rejoice to bring Him to you today, in a new way it may be in some ways—even though it be in my crooked Yorkshire speech—and say to you that He is the only Jesus; He is the only plan; He is the only life; He is the only help. Thank God

He has triumphed to the uttermost. He came to seek and to save that which was lost, and He heals all who come to Him.

As the palsied man was let down through the roof, there was a great commotion, and all the people were gazing up at this strange sight. "When Jesus saw their faith, he said unto the sick of the palsy, 'Son, thy sins are forgiven thee'" (Mk 2:5). What had the forgiveness of sins to do with the healing of this man? It had everything to do with it. Sin is at the root of disease. May the Lord cleanse us from outward sin and inbred sin and take away from us all that hinders the power of God to work through us.

Jesus had seen the weakness and helplessness of that man. He saw also the faith of his four friends. There is something in this for us today. Many people will not be saved unless some of us are used to stir them up. Remember that we are our brother's keeper. We must take our brother or sister in need to Jesus. When these men carried the palsied man, they pressed through until he could hear the voice of the Son of God, and liberty came to the captive. The man became strong by the power of God, arose, took up his bed, and went before them all.

Oh, beloved, I have seen wonderful things like this wrought by the power of God. We must never think about our God on small lines. He spoke the Word one day and made the world of things that had not been. That is the kind of God we have, and He is just the same today. There is no change in Him. He is lovely and precious above all thought and comparison. There is none like Him.

Let us thank the Lord that He is bringing out the gospel as in the days of His flesh. God is working in the midst of us, but I want to know, what are you going to do with the gospel today? There are greater blessings for you than you have ever received in your life. Do you believe it and will you receive it?   *The Anointing of His Spirit*

QUESTIONS TO CONSIDER
1. Is Jesus' healing touch a reality to you? Why or why not?
2. What are you going to do with the gospel today? Be specific.

A PRAYERFUL RESPONSE
Lord, I need and accept Your healing touch. Amen.

A CAUSE FOR PURITY

THOUGHT FOR TODAY

God works through people who stay morally and spiritually pure.

WISDOM FROM SCRIPTURE

But a man named Ananias, with the consent of his wife Sapphira, sold a piece of property; with his wife's knowledge, he kept back some of the proceeds, and brought only a part and laid it at the apostles' feet.

"Ananias," Peter asked, "why has Satan filled your heart to lie to the Holy Spirit and to keep back part of the proceeds of the land?

"While it remained unsold, did it not remain your own? And after it was sold, were not the proceeds at your disposal? How is it that you have contrived this deed in your heart? You did not lie to us but to God!"

Now when Ananias heard these words, he fell down and died. And great fear seized all who heard of it.

The young men came and wrapped up his body, then carried him out and buried him.

After an interval of about three hours his wife came in, not knowing what had happened.

Peter said to her, "Tell me whether you and your husband sold the land for such and such a price." And she said, "Yes, that was the price."

Then Peter said to her, "How is it that you have agreed together to put the Spirit of the Lord to the test? Look, the feet of those who have buried your husband are at the door, and they will carry you out."

Immediately she fell down at his feet and died. When the young men came in they found her dead, so they carried her out and buried her beside her husband.

And great fear seized the whole church and all who heard of these things.

Now many signs and wonders were done among the people through the apostles. And they were all together in Solomon's Portico.

None of the rest dared to join them, but the people held them in high esteem.

Yet more than ever believers were added to the Lord, great numbers of both men and women, so that they even carried out the sick into the streets, and laid them on cots and mats, in order that Peter's shadow might fall on some of them as he came by.

A great number of people would also gather from the towns around Jerusalem, bringing the sick and those tormented by unclean spirits, and they were all cured.

Then the high priest took action; he and all who were with him (that is, the sect of the Sadducees), being filled with jealousy, arrested the apostles and put them in the public prison.

But during the night an angel of the Lord opened the prison doors, brought them out, and said, "Go, stand in the temple and tell the people the whole message about this life."   ACTS 5:1-20, NRSV

INSIGHTS FROM SMITH WIGGLESWORTH

Notice this expression the Lord gives of the gospel message: "the words of this life" (Acts 5:20). It is the most wonderful life possible—the life of faith in the Son of God. This is the life where God is all the time; He is round about and He is within.

It is the life of many revelations and of many manifestations of God's Holy Spirit, a life in which the Lord is continually seen, known, felt, and heard. It would take me months to tell what there is in this wonderful life. Everyone can possess and be possessed by this life.

It is possible to be within the vicinity of this life and yet miss it. It is possible to be in a place where God is pouring out His Spirit and yet miss the blessing He is so willing to bestow. This happens when we misunderstand the infinite grace of the God of all grace, who is willing to give to all who will reach out the hand of faith.

This life He freely bestows is a gift. Some think they have to earn it and they miss the whole thing. Oh, for a simple faith to receive all that God so lavishly offers. You can never be ordinary from the day you receive this life from above. You become extraordinary, filled with the extraordinary power of our extraordinary God.

Ananias and Sapphira were in this thing and yet they missed it. They were in the wonderful revival that God gave the early Church and yet they missed it. There are many people like them today who make vows to God in times of great crisis in their lives. They fail to keep their vows and in the end they become spiritually bankrupt.

Blessed is the person who keeps the vow he has made to God. There is no dry place for such a person; he is always spiritually fat and flourishing, and he becomes stronger and stronger. It pays to trust God with all and to make no reservation. We have a great God.

Ananias and Sapphira were doubting God and questioning whether this work He had begun would continue. They wanted to get some glory for selling their property, but because of their lack of faith they kept back part of the price in reserve in case the work of God should fail.

In the early Church, controlled by the power of the Holy Spirit, it was not possible for a carnal life to exist. The moment it came into the Church, it died instantly. As the power of the Holy Spirit increases in these days of revival, it will be impossible for any person to remain in our midst with a lying spirit. God will purify the Church; the Word of God will be in such power through healing and other supernatural manifestations that great fear will be upon all those who see it.

It seems to the natural mind a small thing for Ananias and Sapphira to want to have a little to fall back on, but we can please God, and get things from God only through a living faith. God never fails. God never can fail.

Ever Increasing Faith

QUESTIONS TO CONSIDER
1. What can you learn from the story of Ananias and Sapphira?
2. What does spiritual purity mean to you?

A PRAYERFUL RESPONSE
Lord, keep my heart and motivations pure before You. Amen.

DAY 34

WILL YOU BE MADE WHOLE?

THOUGHT FOR TODAY

Even if we've missed previous opportunities, Christ wants to make us whole.

WISDOM FROM SCRIPTURE

After this there was a festival of the Jews, and Jesus went up to Jerusalem.

Now in Jerusalem by the Sheep Gate there is a pool, called in Hebrew Beth-zatha, which has five porticoes. In these lay many invalids—blind, lame, and paralyzed.

One man was there who had been ill for thirty-eight years. When Jesus saw him lying there and knew that he had been there a long time, he said to him, "Do you want to be made well?"

The sick man answered him, "Sir, I have no one to put me into the pool when the water is stirred up; and while I am making my way, someone else steps down ahead of me."

Jesus said to him, "Stand up, take your mat and walk."

At once the man was made well, and he took up his mat and began to walk. Now that day was a sabbath.

So the Jews said to the man who had been cured, "It is the sabbath; it is not lawful for you to carry your mat."

But he answered them, "The man who made me well said to me, 'Take up your mat and walk.'"

They asked him, "Who is the man who said to you, 'Take it up and walk'?"

Now the man who had been healed did not know who

it was, for Jesus had disappeared in the crowd that was there.

Later Jesus found him in the temple and said to him, "See, you have been made well! Do not sin any more, so that nothing worse happens to you."

The man went away and told the Jews that it was Jesus who had made him well.

Therefore the Jews started persecuting Jesus, because he was doing such things on the sabbath.

But Jesus answered them, "My Father is still working, and I also am working."

For this reason the Jews were seeking all the more to kill him, because he was not only breaking the sabbath, but was also calling God his own Father, thereby making himself equal to God.

Jesus said to them, "Very truly, I tell you, the Son can do nothing on his own, but only what he sees the Father doing; for whatever the Father does, the Son does likewise.

"The Father loves the Son and shows him all that he himself is doing; and he will show him greater works than these, so that you will be astonished.

"Indeed, just as the Father raises the dead and gives them life, so also the Son gives life to whomever he wishes.

"The Father judges no one but has given all judgment to the Son, so that all may honor the Son just as they honor the Father. Anyone who does not honor the Son does not honor the Father who sent him.

"Very truly, I tell you, anyone who hears my word and believes him who sent me has eternal life, and does not come under judgment, but has passed from death to life."

JOHN 5:1-24, NRSV

There they were around the pool—a multitude of impotent folk, blind and withered, waiting for the moving of the water. Did Jesus heal everybody? He left many around that pool unhealed. There were doubtless many who had their eyes on the pool but had no eyes for Jesus. There are many today who have their confidence in things seen. If they would get their eyes on God instead of natural things, how quickly they would be helped.

The Word can drive every disease away from our bodies. It is our portion in Christ—Him who is our bread, our life, our health, our all in all. And though we may be deep in sin, we can come to Him in repentance and He will forgive, cleanse, and heal us. His words are spirit and life to those who will receive them. The life of Jesus Christ, God's Son, can so purify our hearts and minds that we become entirely transformed in spirit, soul, and body.

There they were around the pool, and one man had been there a long time. His infirmity was of thirty-eight years' standing. Now and again an opportunity would come as the angel stirred the water, but his heart would be made sick as he saw another step in and be healed before him. One day Jesus was passing that way, and seeing him lying there in that sad condition, asked, "Will thou be made whole?" (Jn 5:6) Jesus said it, and His work is from everlasting to everlasting.

This is His word to you today, poor, tired, and tested one. You may say, like this poor, impotent man, "I have missed every opportunity up until now." Never mind about that. Will you be made whole?

I visited a woman who had been suffering for many years. She was twisted with rheumatism and had been in bed for two years. I asked her, "What makes you lie here?"

She said, "I've come to the conclusion that I have a thorn in the flesh."

I said, "To what wonderful degree of righteousness have you attained that you have to have a thorn in the flesh? Have you had such an abundance of divine revelations that there is danger of your being exalted above measure?"

She said, "I believe it is the Lord who is causing me to suffer."

I said, "You believe it is the Lord's will for you to suffer, and you are trying to get out of it as quickly as you can. There are doctors' bottles all over the place. Get out of your hiding place and confess that you are a sinner. If you'll get rid of your self-righteousness, God will do something for you. Drop the idea that you are so holy that God has to afflict you."

There is healing through the blood of Christ and deliverance for every captive. God never intended His children to live in misery because of some affliction that comes directly from the devil. A perfect atonement was made at Calvary. Jesus bore our sins, and we are free from them all. We are justified from all things if we dare believe. He Himself took our infirmities and bore our sicknesses. If we dare believe, we can be healed.

See this poor, helpless man at the pool. "Wilt thou be made whole?" But there is a difficulty in the way. The man has one eye on the pool and one on Jesus. There are many people getting cross-eyed this way these days; they have one eye on the doctor and one on Jesus. If you will only look to Christ and put both your eyes on Him, you can be made every whit whole, spirit, soul, and body. It is the word of the living God that they that believe should be justified, made free from all things. And whom the Son sets free is free indeed.

Ever Increasing Faith

QUESTIONS TO CONSIDER

1. Do you believe God can and will make you whole? Why or why not?
2. How can you bring God's healing and wholeness to others?

A PRAYERFUL RESPONSE

Lord, I am willing to be made whole. But first heal me of my unbelief. Amen.

COUNT IT ALL JOY

THOUGHT FOR TODAY

Trials bring joy because they prove what God can do for us.

WISDOM FROM SCRIPTURE

James, a servant of God and of the Lord Jesus Christ, To the twelve tribes in the Dispersion: Greetings.

My brothers and sisters, whenever you face trials of any kind, consider it nothing but joy, because you know that the testing of your faith produces endurance; and let endurance have its full effect, so that you may be mature and complete, lacking in nothing.

If any of you is lacking in wisdom, ask God, who gives to all generously and ungrudgingly, and it will be given you.

But ask in faith, never doubting, for the one who doubts is like a wave of the sea, driven and tossed by the wind; for the doubter, being double-minded and unstable in every way, must not expect to receive anything from the Lord.

JAMES 1:1-7, NRSV

INSIGHTS FROM SMITH WIGGLESWORTH

James addressed his letter to "the twelve tribes which are scattered abroad" (Jas 1:1). Only one like the Master could stand and say, "My brethren, count it all joy when ye fall into divers temptations" (verse 2). How could James write, "Count it all joy," when they were scattered everywhere? Driven to their wits' end! Persecuted!

The Scriptures say that "they wandered in deserts, and in mountains, and in dens and caves of the earth" (Heb 11:38). His people were scattered abroad, but God was with them. It does not matter where you are if God is with you. He who is for you is a million times more than all who can be against you.

Oh, if we could by the grace of God see that the beatitudes of God's divine power come to us with such sweetness, whispering to us, "Be still, my child. All is well." Only be still and see the salvation of the Lord. What would happen if we learned the secret to ask only once and believe? What an advantage it would be if only we could come to a place where we knew that everything is within our reach. God wants us to see that every obstacle can be moved away.

God brings us into a place where there are difficulties, where there is no pleasure, where there are hard corners. We know there are no possibilities on the human side—God must do it. All these places are of God's ordering. God allows trials, difficulties, temptations, and perplexities to come right along our path, but there is not a temptation or trial that comes to us but that God has a way out. We do not have a way out; it is God who can bring us through!

I would pity a believer who has gone a week without temptation. Why? Because God only tries those who are worthy. You might be passing through difficulties. Trials are rising, darkness is appearing, and everything is becoming so dense you cannot see through it. Hallelujah! God is seeing you through. He is a God of deliverance, a God of power. Oh, He is near to save if you will only believe. He can anoint you with fresh oil; He can make your cup run over. Jesus is the balm of Gilead; yes, the Rose of Sharon.

I believe that God, the Holy Spirit, wants to bring us into line with such perfection of beatitude and beauty that we shall say, "Lord, Lord, though You slay me, yet will I trust You" (Job 13:15). When the hand of God is upon us and the clay is fresh in the Potter's hands, the vessel will be made perfect as we are pliable. Only melted gold is minted; only moistened clay is molded; only softened wax receives the seal; only broken, contrite hearts receive the mark as the Potter turns us on His wheel—shaped and burnt to take and keep the mark, the mold, the stamp of God's pure gold.

God can put the stamp on this day. He can mold us afresh. He can change the vision. He can remove the difficulty. The Lord of Hosts is in our midst and is waiting for our affection. Remember His question: "Simon, son of Jonas, lovest thou me more than these?" (Jn 21:15).

God never lets the chastening rod fall upon anything except what is marring the vessel. If there is anything in us that is not yielded and bent to the plan of the Almighty, we cannot preserve what is spiritual only in part. When the Spirit of the Lord gets perfect control, when we begin to be changed from glory to glory by the expression of God's light in our human frame and our whole body begins to have the fullness of His life manifested in us, God enables us to believe all things.

When God brings us into oneness and fellowship with the Most High God, our nature will quiver in His presence. But He can chase away all the defects, unrest, unfaithfulness, and wavering. He can establish us with such strong consolation that we can just rest there in the Holy Spirit by the power of God—ready to be revealed. God invites us to higher heights and deeper depths.

We can pray these words to God:

Make me better, make me purer,
By the fire which refines,
Where the breath of God is sweeter,
Where the brightest glory shines.
Bring me high up the mountain
Into fellowship with thee,
In thy light I'll see the fountain,
And the blood that cleanses me.

I ask you in the name of Jesus, will you cast all your care upon Him? "For he cares for you" (1 Pt 5:7). Come on, beloved, let us weep together. I believe a real weeping would be good for us. You are in a poor way if you cannot weep. I thank God for my tears; they help me. I like to weep in the presence of God.

God will help us. Glory to God. How He meets the need of the hungry!   *The Anointing of His Spirit*

QUESTIONS TO CONSIDER
1. What trials are you walking through now?
2. How can you allow God to refine you through these trials?

A PRAYERFUL RESPONSE
Lord, make me better and purer with Your refining fire. Amen.

PART FIVE

PRESSING TOWARD THE GOAL

In Switzerland a man attended a church and one morning.
At the breaking of bread service, he arose and said,
"Brethren, we have the Word, and I feel that we are living
    in the letter of it,
but there is a hunger and thirst in my soul for something deeper,
something more real than we have, and I cannot rest
    until we enter into it."
He did this for several weeks until it got on the nerves of those people
and they protested, "Sands, you are making us all miserable.
You are spoiling our meetings, and there is only one thing
    for you to do, and that is to clear out."

So he came to our meetings. He was so hungry and thirsty that he
    drank in every word that was said. After three weeks he said,
"God will have to do something now or I'll burst."
He breathed in God and the Lord filled him.

God is making people hungry and thirsty after His best.
Are you hungry? If you are, God promises that you shall be filled.

FAITH THAT PREVAILS

SMITH WIGGLESWORTH'S INSIGHT

We are to press on until we receive God's answer and blessings.

DAY 36

KEEPING THE VISION

THOUGHT FOR TODAY

Each day we can ask God to keep His vision fresh within us.

WISDOM FROM SCRIPTURE

And you also were included in Christ when you heard the word of truth, the gospel of your salvation. Having believed, you were marked in him with a seal, the promised Holy Spirit, who is a deposit guaranteeing our inheritance until the redemption of those who are God's possession to the praise of his glory.

For this reason, ever since I heard about your faith in the Lord Jesus and your love for all the saints, I have not stopped giving thanks for you, remembering you in my prayers.

I keep asking that the God of our Lord Jesus Christ, the glorious Father, may give you the Spirit of wisdom and revelation, so that you may know him better.

I pray also that the eyes of your heart may be enlightened in order that you may know the hope to which he has called you, the riches of his glorious inheritance in the saints, and his incomparably great power for us who believe. That power is like the working of his mighty strength, which he exerted in Christ when he raised him from the dead and seated him at his right hand in the heavenly realms, far above all rule and authority, power and dominion, and every title that can be given, not only in the present age but also in the one to come.

And God placed all things under his feet and appointed him to be head over everything for the church, which is his body, the fullness of him who fills everything in every way.

EPHESIANS 1:13-23, NIV

INSIGHTS FROM SMITH WIGGLESWORTH

Oh, what condescension that God should lay hold of humanity and so possess it with His holiness, righteousness, truth, and faith, that we can say, "I am bound in spirit; I have no choice; my only choice is for God; my only desire, my only ambition is the will of God; I am bound with God."

Is this possible? If you look into Galatians 1, you will see how wonderfully Paul rose into this state of bliss. If you look in the third chapter of Ephesians, you will see that he recognized himself as less than the least of all saints. Then if you'll look in Acts 26 you will find him saying, "I have never lost the vision, King Agrippa, I have never lost it."

Then if you look again in Galatians, you will see that to keep the vision, he conferred not with flesh and blood; God laid hold of him, God bound him, God preserved him. It is a wonderful position to be in—to be preserved by Almightiness—and we ought to see to it that we give ourselves to God. The consequences will be all right.

I appeal to you who have received the Holy Spirit. I appeal to you to let God have His way at whatever cost. I appeal to you to keep moving on with God into an ever increasing realization of His infinite purpose in Christ Jesus for His redeemed ones until you are filled with all the fullness of God.

The child of God must catch the vision anew every day. Every day the child of God must be moved more and more by the Holy Spirit. The child of God must come into line with the power of heaven so he knows God has His hand upon him.

Jesus went about doing good. Is not that the ministry God would have us be heir to? The mission of the Holy Spirit is to give us a revelation of Jesus and to make the Word of God life to us as it was when spoken by the Son—as new, as fresh, as effective as if the Lord Himself were speaking. The Bride loves to hear the Bridegroom's voice!

Here it is: the blessed Word of God, the whole Word, not part of it, no! We believe in the whole of it. We have such an effectiveness worked in us by the Word of life that day by day we are finding out that the Word itself gives life. The Spirit of the Lord breathes through the Word, giving it afresh to us, making the whole Word alive today.

So I have within my hands, my heart, my mind, this blessed reservoir of promises that is able to do so many marvelous things. Some of you most likely have been suffering because you have a limited revelation of Jesus, of the fullness of life there is in Him.

In Acts 2 we see that when the Holy Spirit came there was such a manifestation of the power of God that it brought conviction as the Word was spoken in the Holy Spirit. In the third chapter we read of the lame man healed at the Beautiful Gate through the power of the Spirit, as Peter and John went into the temple. And in the fourth chapter, we read of such a wonderful manifestation of miraculous power through the Spirit that five thousand men besides women and children became believers in the Lord Jesus Christ.

God gives manifestations of His divine power to prove He is with us. Will you not, right now, open your heart to this wonderful God and let Him come into your life and make of you all that His infinite wisdom has conceived—all that His infinite love has moved Him to provide in Christ Jesus and all that His infinite power, through the Holy Spirit, has made possible to be wrought in sinful man?

See this vision from God and keep it ever before you. Pray the prayer that the Apostle Paul prayed for the Ephesian believers, as recorded in Ephesians 1:17-19: "That the God of our Lord Jesus Christ, the Father of glory, may give unto you a spirit of wisdom and revelation in the knowledge of Him: having the eyes of your heart enlightened, that ye may know what is the hope of His calling, what the riches of the glory of His inheritance in the saints, and what the exceeding greatness of His power to us who believe."

Faith That Prevails

Questions to Consider
1. What spiritual vision has God placed in your heart?
2. How can you bring clarity to this vision?

A Prayerful Response
Lord, keep Your vision fresh within me each day. Amen.

THE WAY TO PRAISE

THOUGHT FOR TODAY

The risen Christ within us prompts us to praise with our hearts and our mouths.

WISDOM FROM SCRIPTURE

Then Peter, filled with the Holy Spirit, said to them: "Rulers and elders of the people!

"If we are being called to account today for an act of kindness shown to a cripple and are asked how he was healed, then know this, you and everyone else in Israel: It is by the name of Jesus Christ of Nazareth, whom you crucified but whom God raised from the dead, that this man stands before you completely healed.

"He is 'the stone you builders rejected, which has become the capstone.'

"Salvation is found in no one else, for there is no other name under heaven given to men by which we must be saved."

When they saw the courage of Peter and John and realized that they were unschooled, ordinary men, they were astonished and they took note that these men had been with Jesus.

But since they could see the man who had been healed standing there with them, there was nothing they could say....

Then they called them in again and commanded them not to speak or teach at all in the name of Jesus.

But Peter and John replied, "Judge for yourselves

whether it is right in God's sight to obey you rather than God.

"For we cannot help speaking about what we have seen and heard."

After further threats they let them go. They could not decide how to punish them, because all the people were praising God for what had happened.

For the man who was miraculously healed was over forty years old.

On their release, Peter and John went back to their own people and reported all that the chief priests and elders had said to them.

When they heard this, they raised their voices together in prayer to God. "Sovereign Lord," they said, "you made the heaven and the earth and the sea, and everything in them.

"You spoke by the Holy Spirit through the mouth of your servant, our father David:

"Why do the nations rage and the peoples plot in vain?

"The kings of the earth take their stand and the rulers gather together against the Lord and against his Anointed One.

"Indeed Herod and Pontius Pilate met together with the Gentiles and the people of Israel in this city to conspire against your holy servant Jesus, whom you anointed.

"They did what your power and will had decided before-hand should happen.

"Now, Lord, consider their threats and enable your servants to speak your word with great boldness.

"Stretch out your hand to heal and perform miraculous signs and wonders through the name of your holy servant Jesus."

After they prayed, the place where they were meeting was shaken. And they were all filled with the Holy Spirit and spoke the word of God boldly.

Acts 4:8-14, 18-31, NIV

Today we praise God for the fact that our glorious Jesus is the risen Christ. Those of us who have tasted the power of the indwelling Spirit know something of the manner in which the hearts of those two disciples burned as they walked to Emmaus with the risen Lord as their Companion.

Note the words of Acts 4:31, "And when they had prayed, the place was shaken." Many churches never pray the kind of prayer we read of here. A church that doesn't now know how to pray and to shout will never be shaken. It is only when people have learned the secret of prayer, of power and of praise, that God comes forth. Some people say, "Well, I praise God inwardly." But if there is an abundance of praise in our hearts, our mouths cannot help speaking it.

There was a man who had a large business in London who was a great churchgoer. The church he attended was beautifully decorated, and his pew was delightfully cushioned—just smooth enough to make it easy to sleep through the sermons. He was a prosperous man in business, but he had no peace in his heart. There was a boy at his business who always looked happy; he was always jumping and whistling.

One day the man said to the boy, "I want to see you in my office."

When the boy was in his office the man asked him, "How is it that you can always whistle and be happy?"

"I cannot help it," answered the boy.

"Where did you get it?" asked the man.

The boy told him and soon he was attending Spirit-filled services. The Lord broke the man up there, and in a short time he was entirely changed. One day shortly after this, he found instead of being distracted by his business as he formerly had been, he was actually whistling and jumping. His whole position and his whole life had been changed.

The shout cannot come out unless it is in. There must first be the inner working of the power of God; it is He who changes the heart and transforms the life. Before there is any real outward evidence there must be the inflow of divine life.

Sometimes I say to people, "You weren't at our meeting the other night."

They reply, "Oh, yes, I was there in spirit."

I say to them, "Well, come next time with your body also. We don't want a lot of spirits here and no bodies. We want you to come and get filled with God."

When all the people will come and pray and praise as the early disciples did there will be something doing. People who come will catch fire and they will want to come again. They will have no use for a place where everything has been formal, dry, and dead.

The power of Pentecost came at first to loose people. God wants to free us in every way. Men and women are tired of imitations; they want reality; they want to see people who have the living Christ within and are filled with the Holy Spirit's power. *Ever Increasing Faith*

QUESTIONS TO CONSIDER
1. How do you feel about praising God out loud?
2. What can you do to cultivate a life of praise to God?

A PRAYERFUL RESPONSE
Lord, I praise You for the risen Christ. Catch me on fire with His power. Amen.

DAY 38

PERFECT REST

THOUGHT FOR TODAY

God invites us to enter daily into His rest.

WISDOM FROM SCRIPTURE

Therefore, since the promise of entering his rest still stands, let us be careful that none of you be found to have fallen short of it.

For we also have had the gospel preached to us, just as they did; but the message they heard was of no value to them, because those who heard did not combine it with faith.

Now we who have believed enter that rest, just as God has said, "So I declared on oath in my anger, 'They shall never enter my rest.'" And yet his work has been finished since the creation of the world.

For somewhere he has spoken about the seventh day in these words: "And on the seventh day God rested from all his work."

And again in the passage above he says, "They shall never enter my rest."

It still remains that some will enter that rest, and those who formerly had the gospel preached to them did not go in, because of their disobedience.

Therefore God again set a certain day, calling it Today, when a long time later he spoke through David, as was said before: "Today, if you hear his voice, do not harden your hearts."

For if Joshua had given them rest, God would not have spoken later about another day.

There remains, then, a Sabbath-rest for the people of God; for anyone who enters God's rest also rests from his own work, just as God did from his.

Let us, therefore, make every effort to enter that rest, so that no one will fall by following their example of disobedience.

For the word of God is living and active. Sharper than any double-edged sword, it penetrates even to dividing soul and spirit, joints and marrow; it judges the thoughts and attitudes of the heart.

Nothing in all creation is hidden from God's sight. Everything is uncovered and laid bare before the eyes of him to whom we must give account.

Therefore, since we have a great high priest who has gone through the heavens, Jesus the Son of God, let us hold firmly to the faith we profess.

For we do not have a high priest who is unable to sympathize with our weaknesses, but we have one who has been tempted in every way, just as we are—yet was without sin.

Let us then approach the throne of grace with confidence, so that we may receive mercy and find grace to help us in our time of need.   HEBREWS 4, NIV

INSIGHTS FROM SMITH WIGGLESWORTH

The Holy Spirit will make the Word powerful in you till every evil thing that presents itself against the obedience and fullness of Christ withers away. I want to show you the need of the baptism of the Holy Spirit, by which you know there is perfect rest when you are filled with the Holy Spirit. I want you to see perfect rest.

I want you to see Jesus. He was filled with the Holy Spirit. The storm began so terribly. The ship filled with water. He lay asleep. Perfect rest. When the disciples cried, "Master, we perish!" Jesus rose, filled with the Holy Spirit, and rebuked the wind and spoke His peace.

I want you to see that this Holy Spirit, this divine Person, has to get so deep into you that He must destroy every evil thing. "For the Word of God is quick, powerful, sharper than any two-edged sword, piercing even to the driving asunder of soul and spirit, and of the joints and marrow" (Heb 4:12).

Some people get pain in their life after being saved because of soulishness. They want to do good but find evil; they continue to do the thing they hate to do. They need the baptism of the Holy Spirit, for then the Holy Spirit will so reveal the Word that it will be like a sword. It will cut between their soul and their spirit until they can no more long for indulgence in things contrary to the mind and will of God.

Don't you want rest? How long will you take to enter that rest? God wants you to enter that rest. Enter into rest, get filled with the Holy Spirit. Your unbelief will depart. Unbelief is sin. It is the greatest sin because it hinders you from all blessings.

My heart is so full of this truth that Jesus is the Word. It takes the Holy Spirit to make the Word active. Jesus is the Word that is mighty by the power of the Spirit to the pulling down of strongholds, moving upon us so that the power of God is seen upon us.

Remember that Jesus is all fullness. Remember Jesus was the fullness of the Godhead. The Holy Spirit makes Him so precious that, "It's all right now, it's all right now, for Jesus is my Savior, and it's all right now."

I want you all to have a share! Oh, for the Holy Spirit to come with freshness upon you; then you all could sing, "It's all right now!" Let me encourage you. God is a God of encouragement.

No creature is hid from His sight, all are naked before Him. When God speaks of nakedness He does not mean that He looks at flesh without clothing. He looks at our spiritual lack and wants us to be clothed with Christ within. He sees our weakness, our sorrow of heart. He is looking right into us now. Oh, what does He see? "Seeing then that we have a great high priest, that is passed into the heavens, Jesus the Son of God, let us hold fast our profession" (Heb 4:14).

What is our profession? I have heard so many people testifying about their profession. Some say, "Thank God He has baptized me with the Holy Spirit." That is my profession; is it yours? That is the profession of the Bible, and God wants to make it your profession.

"There remaineth therefore a rest to the people of God" (Heb 4:9). Some say, "Oh, yes, it is a rest up there." No! The rest is here, when we cease from our own works, this day! If you won't resist the Holy Spirit, the power of God will melt you down. The Holy Spirit will so take charge of you that you will be filled to the uttermost with the overflowing of His grace.

Smith Wigglesworth: A Man Who Walked with God

QUESTIONS TO CONSIDER

1. What does it mean to enter into God's rest?
2. If you entered into God's rest, how might it change your daily life?

A PRAYERFUL RESPONSE

Lord, I long to enter into Your rest. Teach me how to rest in You. Amen.

PRESENT-TIME BLESSINGS

THOUGHT FOR TODAY

God's blessings are more satisfying than the world's rewards.

WISDOM FROM SCRIPTURE

Now when he saw the crowds, he went up on a mountainside and sat down. His disciples came to him, and he began to teach them, saying:

"Blessed are the poor in spirit, for theirs is the kingdom of heaven.

"Blessed are those who mourn, for they will be comforted.

"Blessed are the meek, for they will inherit the earth.

"Blessed are those who hunger and thirst for righteousness, for they will be filled.

"Blessed are the merciful, for they will be shown mercy.

"Blessed are the pure in heart, for they will see God.

"Blessed are the peacemakers, for they will be called sons of God.

"Blessed are those who are persecuted because of righteousness, for theirs is the kingdom of heaven.

"Blessed are you when people insult you, persecute you and falsely say all kinds of evil against you because of me.

"Rejoice and be glad, because great is your reward in heaven, for in the same way they persecuted the prophets who were before you."

MATTHEW 5:1-12

* * *

"Come, all you who are thirsty, come to the waters; and you who have no money, come, buy and eat! Come, buy wine and milk without money and without cost.

"Why spend money on what is not bread, and your labor on what does not satisfy? Listen, listen to me, and eat what is good, and your soul will delight in the richest of fare.

"Give ear and come to me; hear me, that your soul may live. I will make an everlasting covenant with you, my faithful love promised to David.

"See, I have made him a witness to the peoples, a leader and commander of the peoples.

"Surely you will summon nations you know not, and nations that do not know you will hasten to you, because of the LORD your God, the Holy One of Israel, for he has endowed you with splendor."

Seek the LORD while he may be found; call on him while he is near.

Let the wicked forsake his way and the evil man his thoughts. Let him turn to the LORD, and he will have mercy on him, and to our God, for he will freely pardon.

"For my thoughts are not your thoughts, neither are your ways my ways," declares the LORD.

ISAIAH 55:1-8, NIV

INSIGHTS FROM SMITH WIGGLESWORTH

In Matthew 5 the Lord Jesus sets forth present-day blessings that we can enjoy here and now.

"Blessed are the poor in spirit, for theirs is the kingdom of heaven" (Mt 5:3). This is one of the richest places into which Jesus brings us. The poor have a right to everything in heaven. Dare we believe it?

Yes, I dare. I believe. I know I was very poor. When God's

Spirit comes in as the ruling, controlling power of our life, He gives us God's revelation of our inward poverty and shows us that God has come with one purpose: to bring heaven's best to earth. In Jesus He will indeed freely give us all things.

An old man and woman had lived together for seventy years. Someone said to them, "You must have seen many clouds during those days." They replied, "Where do the showers come from? You never get showers without clouds."

It is only the Holy Spirit who can bring us to the place where we realize our poverty; but every time He does it, He opens the windows of heaven and the showers of blessing fall.

"Blessed are they that mourn: for they shall be comforted" (vs 4). There is a mourning in the Spirit. God brings us to a place where things must be changed, and there is a mourning, an unutterable groaning until God comes. But the end of all real faith always is rejoicing. Jesus mourned over Jerusalem. He saw the conditions; He saw the unbelief; He saw the end of those who close their ears to the gospel. But God promised that He would see the travails of His soul be satisfied, and that He would see His seed.

What happened on the day of Pentecost in Jerusalem was a taste of what the results of His travail will be, to be multiplied a billionfold down through the ages. And as we enter in the Spirit into travail over conditions that are wrong, such mourning will bring results for God, and our joy will be complete in the satisfaction that is brought to Christ.

"Blessed are the meek: for they shall inherit the earth" (vs 5). Moses was headstrong in his zeal for his own people, and it resulted in his killing a man. His heart was right in his desire to correct things, but he was working on natural lines, and when we work on natural lines we always fail. Moses had a mighty passion, and that is one of the best things in the world when God has control and it becomes a passion for souls to be born again; but apart from God it is one of the worst things.

Paul had it to a tremendous extreme and, breathing out threats, he was hauling men and women to prison. But God changed him, and later we find him wishing himself accursed from Christ for the sake of his brethren.

God took the headstrong Moses and molded him into the meekest of people. He took the fiery Saul of Tarsus and made him the foremost exponent of grace. God can transform us in like manner, and plant in us a divine meekness and every other thing we lack.

"Blessed are they which do hunger and thirst after righteousness: for they shall be filled" (vs 6). Note the word, *shall* be filled. If you see a "shall" in the Bible, make it yours. Meet the conditions and God will fulfill His word to you.

The Spirit of God is crying, "Ho, every one that thirsteth, come ye to the waters, and he that hath no money; come ye, buy and eat; yea, come, buy wine and milk without money and without price" (Is 55:1). The Spirit of God will take the things of Christ and show them to you that you may have a longing for Christ in His fullness; and when there is that longing, God will not fail to fill you.

Are you thirsty today? The living Christ still invites you to Himself, and I want to testify that He still satisfies the thirsty soul and still fills the hungry with good things. God is making people hunger and thirst after His best. And everywhere He is filling the hungry and giving them what the disciples received at the beginning.

Are you hungry? If you are, God promises that you shall be filled. *Faith That Prevails*

QUESTIONS TO CONSIDER
1. For what do you hunger and thirst today?
2. What will you do to be filled with God?

A PRAYERFUL RESPONSE
Lord, fill my hungry, thirsty soul with You. Amen.

DAY 40

LIVELY HOPE

Our spiritual inheritance in Christ gives us hope.

WISDOM FROM SCRIPTURE

Praise be to the God and Father of our Lord Jesus Christ! In his great mercy he has given us new birth into a living hope through the resurrection of Jesus Christ from the dead, and into an inheritance that can never perish, spoil or fade—kept in heaven for you...

Concerning this salvation, the prophets, who spoke of the grace that was to come to you, searched intently and with the greatest care, trying to find out the time and circumstances to which the Spirit of Christ in them was pointing when he predicted the sufferings of Christ and the glories that would follow.

It was revealed to them that they were not serving themselves but you, when they spoke of the things that have now been told you by those who have preached the gospel to you by the Holy Spirit sent from heaven. Even angels long to look into these things.

Therefore, prepare your minds for action; be self-controlled; set your hope fully on the grace to be given you when Jesus Christ is revealed.

As obedient children, do not conform to the evil desires you had when you lived in ignorance.

But just as he who called you is holy, so be holy in all you do; for it is written: "Be holy, because I am holy."

Since you call on a Father who judges each man's work

impartially, live your lives as strangers here in reverent fear.

For you know that it was not with perishable things such as silver or gold that you were redeemed from the empty way of life handed down to you from your forefathers, but with the precious blood of Christ, a lamb without blemish or defect.

He was chosen before the creation of the world, but was revealed in these last times for your sake.

Through him you believe in God, who raised him from the dead and glorified him, and so your faith and hope are in God.

Now that you have purified yourselves by obeying the truth so that you have sincere love for your brothers, love one another deeply, from the heart.

For you have been born again, not of perishable seed, but of imperishable, through the living and enduring word of God.

1 Peter 1:3-4, 10-23, NIV

INSIGHTS FROM SMITH WIGGLESWORTH

Lively hope! We cannot pass that, because this sanctification of the Spirit brought us into this wonderful position of the glory of God. I want to keep before us the glory of it, the joy of it: a lively hope. A lively hope is exactly opposite of dead!

Lively hope is movement.

Lively hope is looking into.

Lively hope is pressing into.

Lively hope is leaving everything behind you.

Lively hope is keeping the vision.

Lively hope sees Him coming!

Lively hope, we live in it! We are not trying to make ourselves feel that we believe. The lively hope is ready, waiting, filled with the joy and expectation of the King. Praise the Lord!

I want you to know that God has this in mind for you. If you possess it, you will love others toward God. They will see the joy of expectation that comes forth with manifestation, then realization. Pray that God, the Holy Spirit, will move you this way.

Come now, beloved, I want to raise your hopes into such activity, into such joyful experience, that you will have joy to walk if you cannot run!

I trust you will be so reconciled to God that there is not one thing that would interfere with your having this lively hope. If you have any love for the world you cannot have it, because Jesus is not coming for the world. He is coming to the heavenlies, and all the heavenlies are going to Him. There is nothing but joy there! The pride of life is contrary to lively hope because of the greatness of the glories of eternity, which are placed before Him with exceeding joy.

How God loves us, hovers over us, rejoices in us. Our cup is full and running over. The joy of the Lord is our strength. We have a right to be in these glorious places. It is the purpose of God for our souls. We have a right "to an inheritance incorruptible, and undefiled, and that fadeth not away, reserved in heaven" for us (1 Pt 1:4).

First, incorruptible. Second, undefiled. Third, fadeth not away. Fourth, reserved in heaven for us. Glory to God! I tell you it is great, very great. May the Lord help us thirst after this glorious life of Jesus. It is more than new wine. The Holy Spirit is the manifestation of the glories of the new creation, an inheritance incorruptible.

Incorruptible is one of those delightful words God wants all the saints to grasp—everything corruptible, everything seen, fades away. Incorruptible is that which is eternal, ever-lasting, divine, and spiritual. It brings us to a place where God is in the midst of us. And this is only one part of our inheritance in the Spirit. Oh, how beautiful, perfected for ever! No spot, no wrinkle, holy, absolutely pure, all traces of sin withered.

Beloved, God means it for us. Every soul must reach out to this ideal. God has ten thousand more thoughts for us than we have for ourselves. The grace of God is going to move us on to an inheritance incorruptible that fadeth not away.

Fadeth not away! What a heaven of bliss, what a joy of delight, what a foretaste of heaven on earth. Cheerfully go to the work you have to do, because tomorrow you will be in the presence of the King, with the Lord forever and an inheritance that fadeth not away.

Smith Wigglesworth: A Man Who Walked with God

QUESTIONS TO CONSIDER

1. How would you describe your incorruptible spiritual inheritance?
2. What can you do to cultivate a lively hope for this inheritance?

A PRAYERFUL RESPONSE

Lord, thank You for my incorruptible spiritual inheritance. Amen.

Books about Smith Wigglesworth
Baptized by Fire: The Life of Smith Wigglesworth
Smith Wigglesworth: A Life Ablaze with the Power of God
Smith Wigglesworth: Apostle of Faith
Smith Wigglesworth Remembered
Smith Wigglesworth: The Secret of His Power
The Life of Smith Wigglesworth
Wigglesworth: A Man Who Loved God

Compilations of Smith Wigglesworth's Sermons
Cry of the Spirit
Dare to Believe
Ever Increasing Faith
Faith That Prevails
Only Believe!
The Anointing of His Spirit

About the Compiler

With the *Life Messages of Great Christians* series, Judith Couchman hopes you'll be encouraged and enlightened by people who've shared their spiritual journeys through the printed word.

Judith owns Judith & Company, an editorial consulting and writing business. She was the creator and founding editor-in-chief of *Clarity* magazine, managing editor of *Christian Life,* editor of *Sunday Digest,* director of communications for The Navigators, and director of new product development for NavPress.

Besides speaking to women's and professional groups, Judith has published fourteen books and many magazine articles. In addition, she has received numerous awards for her work in secondary education, religious publishing, and corporate communications.

She lives in Colorado.